Ready to Rise

Ready to Rise

Learn How to Elevate Your Energy, Achieve Your Goals and Realize Your Freedom to Live Your Life by Your Own Design.
Upgrade Your System, Upgrade Your Life.

Renee Russo

©2024 All Rights Reserved. No portion of this book may be reproduced, stored in a retrieval system, or transmitted in any form or by any means-electronic, mechanical, photocopy, recording, scanning, or other-except for brief quotations in critical reviews or articles without the prior permission of the author.

Published by Game Changer Publishing

Paperback ISBN: 978-1-965653-76-0
Hardcover ISBN: 978-1-965653-05-0
Digital ISBN: 978-1-965653-06-7

www.GameChangerPublishing.com

DEDICATION

To my mother Leeanne,

Thank you for always being my beacon of light and keeper of hope during my most challenging and excruciating days on my personal journey. Mom, you have been the most consistent source of love and light in my life, for which I am eternally grateful.

As a child, you loved me with compassion and earnestness, showing me respect, patience, and acceptance at every stage of my life. When I left home at 19 to explore the world, you honored my wishes and let me go, even though it meant bearing your own pain and suffering. Despite your fears for me and your own deep sadness, you stood by my decision to roam and honored my wishes. All along, you gave me the most powerful gift of all—my freedom.

Mom, you have become the most loving, generous, and kind grandmother imaginable to your five beautiful grandchildren. Each of them adores and loves you just as much as I do. It is so wonderful to watch you engage with each of your grandchildren at the deepest level of love and care for their unique personalities and needs. Even from across the ocean, they know that you love them endlessly and that you spend every minute of every day sending them your loving energy.

Thank you for being such a wonderful role model for me in all of your community service over the years, both in your work and also your personal time. You have always gone to great lengths to make the world a better place. Through your example, I have found my motivation to give and serve others in the form of this book and my *Life By Design* workshops. I aspire to be the level of servant human that you are.

In honor of your love, grace, and kindness, I dedicate this book to you, my dear mother. I hope that you will allow yourself to receive this praise and recognition because you deserve it and so much more. The light in me sees and honors the light in you, Mom. Thank you, I love you.

– Renee

Read This First

As I say, vision plus execution equals freedom. To help you maximize your return on investment from the purchase of this book and the time you will spend reading it, I would like to extend to you three (3) free gifts to help you get started on your personal transformation journey.

By scanning the QR code below, you will find a complete downloadable companion guide that will provide you with all of the tools, disciplines, and coaching guidance shared with you throughout the book to get your journey started.

Additionally, I have included a digital mini-course to complement the companion guide to ensure that you understand where to start and how to implement the tools and disciplines featured in these pages.

Lastly, I have included the My Life Assessment bonus tool to help you step out of your current system, assess the strength of your Energy Management System, and identify opportunities to upgrade both your system and your life using my simple, practical, and proven methodology.

Unlock your free gifts today!

Scan the QR Code Here:

Ready to Rise

Learn How to Elevate Your Energy, Achieve Your Goals and Realize Your Freedom to Live Your Life by Your Own Design

Upgrade Your System, Upgrade Your Life

Renee Russo

www.GameChangerPublishing.co

Foreword

By Jonathan Smith

I've known Renee for years, and let me tell you, she's the real deal. As the CEO and Founder of Rise Up Business Coaching Solutions Ltd., Renee has spent years in the trenches with business owners, helping them navigate the complex world of entrepreneurship and move toward their goals in business and in life. Her credentials as a Certified Exit Planning Advisor (CEPA) and Expert EOS Implementer® are impressive, but what really sets Renee apart is her personal journey and the profound human being she has become.

Renee's story is one of transformation and triumph. She's faced the kind of challenges that would make most people throw in the towel. A "double exit" from both her marriage and business, then the breakdown of her family and becoming homeless! That's the kind of experience that either breaks you or makes you unstoppable. For Renee, it was the latter.

Throughout this book, Renee shares her *Ready to Rise Energy Management System* and teaches readers how to implement the simple, practical, and proven system as a practical field guide for personal transformation. This isn't just another self-help book or business improvement guide. It's a comprehensive approach to help people reclaim their identity, manage their energy, redesign their life, and get what they really want—their freedom!

As someone who's spent decades working with entrepreneurs myself, I can tell you that every business owner and, frankly, every human that I have met struggles with managing their energy and the common struggles of fatigue, frustration, and fear that come along with that. Now, they have a guidebook to help them get unstuck and achieve the level of freedom they sought when they began their entrepreneurial journey.

What I love about Renee's approach is that it's all about empowerment. She's not here to tell you what to do or how to live your life. Instead, she gives you the tools to become your own coach, or as she puts it, "Guru." Her methodology helps you to take control of your circumstances, make intentional choices, and redesign your life to get what you want personally and professionally.

The energy management system Renee introduces is particularly powerful because it is so simple and practical to integrate; you don't need to go to a workshop or pay an expensive coach—you can do it yourself. In my experience, energy is the currency of entrepreneurship. It's not just about time management or productivity hacks; moreover, when energy is managed well, it can truly help people achieve more with less effort and take the quality of their lives to the next level. Renee's system provides practical tools and disciplines to help readers elevate their energy and live the life they desire.

Renee's book *Ready to Rise* isn't just about theory. Renee has packed this book with actionable insights and tools that you can start using immediately. Whether you're just starting out on your personal development path or you're well on your journey, you'll find value on every page that will help you unlock new levels of capacity and confidence.

What really stands out to me is Renee's authenticity. She's not afraid to share her own struggles and setbacks. This isn't a book written by someone who's had an easy ride to the top. It's written by someone who's faced adversity head-on and come out stronger. That kind of real-world experience is invaluable.

As you read this book, you'll feel like you're sitting down with Renee for a one-on-one coaching session. Her warmth, wisdom, and no-nonsense approach shine through on every page. She has a unique ability to break down complex concepts into simple, actionable steps and empower people to take action. If you are ready for change in your life, I am sure that Renee's words will resonate with you and get you on your path toward positive change.

One of the aspects of this book that I appreciate most is the importance that this content places on aligning the personal, financial, and business priorities of the reader. Too often, entrepreneurs focus solely on growing their businesses without considering their personal freedoms of time and wealth. Renee's approach bridges that gap between the personal and business priorities of the entrepreneur, ensuring that there is a strong focus on wealth creation and financial independence.

The section on creating personal clarity is another highlight. In my work with entrepreneurs, I've found that personal vision clarity is often the missing ingredient for success and fulfillment. Renee provides a roadmap for gaining that clarity, helping you align your personal and professional goals to elevate the sense of purpose and intrinsic rewards from all aspects of life.

Ready to Rise is more than just a book—it's an invitation to transform your life and business. It's about rising above your current circumstances, breaking through limitations, and achieving the kind of success that brings true fulfillment that everyone deserves to have in their life.

If you're an entrepreneur who is ready to take charge of your destiny, this book is for you. If you're tired of feeling stuck or overwhelmed, this book is for you. If you're ready to design a life and business that aligns with your deepest values and aspirations, this book is definitely for you.

Renee Russo has created something special with *Ready to Rise*. It's a testament to her expertise, her passion for helping entrepreneurs, and her own journey of growth and transformation. I'm confident that the strategies and insights in this book will help you achieve new levels of success and fulfillment.

So, are you *Ready to Rise*? Turn the page and let Renee be your guide on this exciting journey that awaits you. Your future self will thank you for it.

Testimonials

"Renee's passion for helping business owners unlock their wealth and achieve their freedom in life is known and trusted by everyone she encounters."

Scott Snider
President, Exit Planning Institute

"Renee's words help people to simplify complexity and remove barriers to give them the confidence to effect meaningful changes in their lives and rise to their higher potential."

Gino Wickman
Author of Traction & Shine,
Creator of EOS®

Table of Contents

Author's Note 1
Introduction 3
Chapter 1 – The Final Fall 11
Chapter 2 – The Climb Up 19
Chapter 3 – Breaking The Pattern 31
Chapter 4 – Building Energy 43
Chapter 5 – Start with Focus 55
Chapter 6 – Planning To Succeed 65
Chapter 7 – Making Progress 77
Chapter 8 – Becoming Myself 85
Chapter 9 – Life By Design 95
Chapter 10 – A System For Living 109
Chapter 11 – Embracing Freedom 121
Chapter 12 – Becoming Selfish 133
Chapter 13 – Helping Others Rise 139
Chapter 14 – Pulling It All Together 145
Chapter 15 – Getting Started 149
Chapter 16 – Self Assessment 153
Conclusion 159
Appendix 165
About the Author 169
Acknowledgments 171

AUTHOR'S NOTE

A series of life events have brought you to this intersection in your life where you now find yourself in the midst of a personal or professional transition, and you are starting to ask yourself some important life questions: *Who am I? Where am I going? What do I want? Will I ever be free?* Do any of these sound familiar? If so, you are in the right place, at the right time, with the right help here at your fingertips.

As you turn through these pages, I will share with you my very own personal story and reveal all of the tools and disciplines I used to help me manage my energy, accelerate my transformation, and realize my freedom to live my *Significant Life* by my own design.

As I say often, upgrade your system, upgrade your life. With the help of the *Ready to Rise Energy Management system*, I am confident that you will find the answers to all of the questions that you are asking yourself and transform your life from the inside out.

There is a summit with your name on it—when you are *Ready to Rise*.

I'll meet you there!

INTRODUCTION

I have been running from myself my entire life, hiding behind the needs of others and doing everything I could do to seek love and acceptance anywhere I could find it. Though, no matter how hard I tried and how far I traveled, I never felt like I was enough, and worse yet, I never felt that I was worthy of the very thing I was chasing—love. In my endeavor to find love and belonging in the world around me, I abandoned my true self out of fear and rejection. For 40 years, I remained hidden behind the facade of a people-pleasing, overly servant, hyper-achieving persona with a perfectly architected smile that had the world convinced that I was happy.

While on the outside I behaved as though everything was great, my inner reality was far from it. In fact, I spent most of my life in a state of inner despair, self-disgust, and complete disconnection from the life I had created. Then, finally, at the age of 40, I could no longer hold up the external production that everything was fine. The truth was that nothing was fine, and I could not fake it anymore.

At last, I cracked; I let go of the facade I had been holding up for so long. I stopped running from myself. I stopped hiding in the needs of others. I just could not do it anymore. The real me that lay hidden deep inside was fighting her way out, whether I liked it or not. She was determined to own her truth and break free of the internal prison she had been held captive in for decades. She wanted out—she wanted to be free.

The decision to leave my marriage was the hardest decision I had made in my entire life. After 15 years of commitment to creating a life together, raising a family, and building a business together, it seemed unfathomable that I would seek to leave the marriage, but the truth was that I was falling apart on the inside, and in order to save myself, I had to bring it to an end. Then, in that single decision to own my truth that I was not happy and pursue my freedom, I lost everything. As my world fell apart right in front of me, a tidal wave of my past pain and suppressed emotions overcame me and sent me into a sharp downward spiral.

This was not my first difficult fall along my life journey. However, it was the most devastating one of all and one that caused me to question whether I would survive the crash. Throughout my life, I pursued many successful peaks of performance personally, academically, and professionally in an effort to prove myself to others, and then, sadly, each one of them was quickly followed by a difficult fall from grace and a lot of hardship. It seemed that as soon as I reached the summit of accomplishment, I would then crash and fall. Rather than stop to figure out what was going on and get professional help, I chose to run faster and work harder, never stopping to address the failure and my inner struggles. I told myself that it was best for everyone if I kept my pain to myself and moved forward to the next opportunity to please others, hoping that one day I could stop chasing happiness and finally experience it.

As I sat in the ruins of my personal life collapse in 2021, having lost my marriage, my family, my community, and my home, I realized that I had nowhere to run to, nowhere to hide, and no one left to please. On some level, I knew it was time to stop running, own up to my inner struggles, and face the reality of my circumstances, but it was not going to be easy.

With nowhere left to run toward, I instead chose to run away from my pain into an unhealthy series of numbing vices that triggered a period of reckless behavior. I shopped excessively, stayed in hotels unnecessarily, drank too much, and soothed myself to sleep with cannabis far too often. No matter how hard I tried to take the edge off and ease my suffering, every morning, I would wake up to the nightmare of my circumstances all over again.

In losing my entire world and everything I valued, I was also stripped of all of the versions of myself that I thought I was. All the external layers of myself that I had built up for the sake of others and to hold up the false facade were removed. Although harsh, this awareness helped me to realize that the only thing I had not yet tried was to be my true self and pursue my own path to happiness—on my own terms. My challenge was I had been locked up inside for so long that I could barely remember who I was and what I wanted in life. I had abandoned myself for so long that I didn't even know how to love and take care of myself anymore. Not only was I displaced in my life, but I was completely lost within myself; getting through this was going to be the biggest fight of my life.

As I sat with the overwhelming reality of being lost and alone, I was reminded of important lessons I had been taught more than a decade prior by my yoga teacher trainer and spiritual guru, Shakti Mhi. I had signed up for the yoga teacher training program after experiencing some tough times during my first year living in Canada. My hope was that the training would help me to ground myself, heal through my struggles, and reconnect with a deeper spiritual path. Though, at the time, the lessons I learned were helpful, it was not until years later that they really came in handy.

In 2006, within months of arriving in Canada to start a life with my then-boyfriend, we had the most devastating diagnosis: he had cancer. From that moment on, everything shifted. Our world flipped upside down, and we went from living in a space of fun and possibilities for our future, into fear and survival mode. We battled through his treatments for months; the experience tested us both and pushed the limits of our relationship.

Fortunately, he survived and healed according to the doctor's plans. Everyone around us celebrated the outcome, and we were both relieved for the fight to be over. Although I, too, was relieved and pleased with the outcome, my challenge was that I struggled to let go of the traumatic experience and had difficulty moving forward. As his primary caregiver, I had taken on a great deal of emotional load that then triggered post-traumatic stress disorder and a very difficult time for me. When I expressed my desire for help, he was not a fan of the idea because he did not want the "quacks" sticking their nose into our lives and quickly shut down the idea. Without any professionals to talk to, I sought an alternative healing approach—yoga.

On the first day of the yoga teacher training program, our guru, Shakti Mhi, stood before the class. She wore long, burgundy robes and had the most powerful presence about her. I could not wait to hear her speak. Then, as she addressed the room of eager students, the first words that came out of her mouth were, "I am not your guru. You may have thought that I was going to heal you or save you, but you are wrong. Instead, I am going to show you how to access your inner power and become your own guide on your healing journey, because you are the guru."

At the time, I experienced a mix of disappointment, rejection, and frustration because I thought that she was going to be the "knower of all things" and provide the answer to all my problems. I had myself convinced that she would save me, but it turned out that I was going to need to learn to do that for myself.

Over the course of our 200 hours of yoga teacher training together, Shakti gave me the tools of movement, breath, and meditation that I needed to guide myself through my post-traumatic stress healing journey. The practices helped me to find deeper inner strength and harness my self-healing capabilities. Though helpful at the time, it turned out that the real power of Shakti's teachings would not come forth until many years later when my world fell apart.

As I looked around at the ruins of my personal life during my divorce proceedings, at last, Shakti's voice and teachings rang true. No one would be able to save me; I would need to find the inner strength and courage to break my patterns and chart a healthier path forward. Once and for all, it was time to become my own Guru.

Although I knew I was ready for change and I had a good set of resources I could draw upon, I quickly became overwhelmed by all of the things that needed to be done and struggled to know where to start. I stalled and stumbled around for some time and felt frustrated by my lack of progress. At times, I doubted whether I had it in me to make it through. Fortunately, as my insecurities started to creep in, I had the benefit of a life-and-death wake-up call one Christmas morning that jolted me into action. In saving the life of another human being on the cold streets of Vancouver that day, I realized that I was not ready to let go of this life and that I had a life worth fighting for. Yes, I had a lot of work to do, and yes, it would be difficult, but the guru in me was ready to come into form; it was my time to rise.

From that moment on, I made the conscious decision to give myself permission to get back up and succeed in life. I committed to stop hiding myself away in shame and guilt and, at last, become my true self. I promised myself that I would build a life that I desired and achieve genuine happiness, once and for all, on my own terms. At long last, I was ready to embrace my freedom to live my life for my own sake and by my own design.

It was not an easy climb out of my darkness to pursue my path to freedom. However, after many months of excruciating effort and a complete shift in my way of thinking, behaving, and managing my energy, I slowly built the capacity to take control of my circumstances and turn my life around for the better.

When I first broke away from my marriage, I craved freedom. Not only freedom from my circumstances but the freedom to be my real self. Then, over time, as I went deeper into my energy management practice, the concept of freedom took on a whole new definition. With practice and intention, freedom became my way of living. I allowed myself to choose to live with purpose in everything I did and say no to things that did not align; I allowed myself to embrace loving relationships with people who loved me as my true self; I opened myself up to perpetual learning and growth to access my higher potential; I welcomed in an abundance of wealth and resources to allow me to live well and contribute to others; and I prioritized my health and holistic well-being each and every day. This freedom to live my life by my own design later became what I then termed my *Significant Life* definition.

In writing this book, I wanted to ensure that it would not end up being simply a story about me, nor did I want it to be the type of book that tells you all the things you *should* do to navigate change in your life, and then leaves you wondering *how* to do it. Instead, my intentions in sharing this book all along have been to, first, be open about my personal struggles in life to help you see that you are not alone in your struggles; second, to share with you the practical tools and disciplines I used to reclaim myself and my life; and third, to give you hope and confidence that with a simple and practical framework, you too can become your own guru and live your *Significant Life.*

If you are feeling stuck in your circumstances and locked up inside of yourself; if you are navigating a personal or professional transition and feel lost; if you have found yourself in a life that doesn't fuel you and you want out, please know that you are not alone and the inner battle that you are likely experiencing is the sign of your inner calling for change. I need you to hear this: *you don't suck—you are just stuck.* Your struggles are symptoms that you are in a transitional period where your old self and new self are at war with one another. You are being called to take action and although it seems hard, you can absolutely do this. If I can do it, you can do it too.

Though you may have tried many different approaches to self-development in the past, I'm guessing that if you are reading this book, chances are you may have hit a ceiling and possibly even feel like nothing is working. The bad news is that this is a crappy place to be in, and it is likely playing with your head. The good news is that you can change your circumstances if you are ready to take ownership of the fact that you are the problem and you need to change. Now, that may sound harsh, I agree, but in reality, the path to change starts right here, within you!

To be clear, I am not prescribing a list of more things that you *should* do. What I intend to do is to help you embrace a simpler, easier, and more effective way to get what you want in life. With the power of a small number of energy management practices and systems intelligence, I hope to make this work so darn easy that you would be crazy not to do it. Throughout the pages of this book, I will share in detail the *5-5-5 Playbook* that I used to heal myself and turn my circumstances around for the better.

In the chapters ahead, I will teach you how to use the simple *5 Rules, 5 Habits,* and *5 Tools* in a systemized world of 90-day planning and execution within the playbook to help you build a strong and sustainable personal energy management practice that will help you become your own guru and, in time, embrace your freedom to live your own version of your *Significant Life.*

Now, if you're not quite ready to go all the way in on this work right now, that's okay. You may simply like to start by using this framework to assess your current practices and figure out what is working for you and what is not. If perhaps you decide that you would like to trial some of the tools and disciplines and see how they impact your day-to-day life, then go right ahead. The resources here are designed to work in part or in full; you can decide for yourself how deep and how quickly you want to go.

Note, if you are a hyper-achiever like me and decide that you want to implement the whole framework, I encourage you to take it slow and keep it simple at first. You can keep coming back to the book and the accompanying resources provided as you need them. All I ask is that you do your best to trust the process, take it one step at a time, and keep moving forward no matter how uncomfortable it may get.

No matter what stage you are at on your personal development journey or how significant the transition you are working through, it is my hope that the insights you gain from reading this book will help you build the courage and the confidence that you can do this, you are worthy, and you are *Ready to Rise.*

CHAPTER 1

THE FINAL FALL

In my lifelong search for love and acceptance, I have sought praise, recognition, and validation from a long list of people and a range of different places. My parents, teachers, coaches, friends, lovers—anyone and everyone. The harder I worked to satisfy others, the more I became a hyper-achieving, people-pleasing, dopamine-addict hooked on the habit of proving myself to others. As I poured all of my energy into serving the interests of others, I worked hard to uphold a strong and positive exterior to convince the world that I was "happy," when the truth was that I was far from happy on the inside. Behind the facade, I experienced crushing depression, self-disgust, and complete disconnection from the life I had created.

This diametric existence of disconnect between my inner experience of despair and outer false representation of joy became my normal, and I worked hard to hide my inner suffering from others. Although maintaining the false front of a perfectly happy life was challenging, the thought of owning my truth was so terrifying that I chose to suppress it and keep my secret to myself. It was here that I held myself captive for 40 years—in denying my truth, I sacrificed my freedom to be my whole and true self.

On the outside, I painted a perfectly crafted smile on my face and convinced everyone that I was happy and achieving everything I had ever wanted in life. I accomplished top marks in school, earned athletic awards, was accepted into a top university, got a revered corporate job, built a perfect little family with my husband... so on and so on. Though on the outside it seemed that I was crushing life, the truth was that I felt empty and lost on the inside. I was making everyone else happy, but I didn't feel that way internally; frankly, I didn't even know who I was or what happiness meant to me.

My fear of rejection and the unrelenting search for connection kept me chasing external validation throughout my entire life. The more I gave to the outside world, the more I needed to sacrifice myself, and, over time, I became a shell of a person with a strong exterior and a completely empty interior. This inner void became a black hole that I tried to fill with endless people-pleasing and a long list of achievements. This became my pattern and my entire way of being for decades. No one else knew about my inner struggles because as soon as they would start to ask questions about me, I would quickly distract them by turning the light on them and focusing my efforts on giving them what they wanted.

The more I pressed forward from one person or project to the next, the further I moved away from my true sense of self and my own identity; I lived in a codependent way to the extent that I lived completely for the sake of others. The bigger the challenge and the greater the opportunity to prove myself, the harder I would push myself to achieve the desired result. In everything I did, I poured myself into it fully. My dad would say, "A job is not worth doing unless it is done well," and, as a byproduct of that, I held myself to the highest standard and never settled for anything less than my absolute best.

The further I went down this path, the more I outsourced responsibility for my happiness to others. I told myself that if I made others happy, then one day, I would feel satisfied and find peace. Then each time when I came up feeling empty, I told myself that I needed to do better and try harder. These rules and conditions I placed on myself held me in this nasty cycle of hyper-achievement for decades. It was not until my final fall that I understood that this way of living was destined for disaster.

Along my path, there were signs that my approach was not ideal and certainly not sustainable, but I chose not to listen to them. Each and every time that I rose to the highs of achievement and reached the summit, I would then crash at the eleventh hour or shortly after having completed the goal. Burnout is the word that I now use to describe these crashes. Back then, I didn't have the language for it or the wherewithal to intervene and get help. Instead, I focused my efforts on covering my tracks and moving on quickly to the next big goal. I thought I could outrun my problems; however, I did not account for all of the emotional baggage I was accumulating along the way, which would eventually catch up with me.

I had risen and fallen academically, athletically, and professionally so many times in my adolescence and young adulthood. After running out of goals to chase and people to please, I went looking for the next challenge and soon found it at 25 years old—marriage. As I came into adulthood, I was exposed to the common societal pressures that all young women experience: the need to marry, have children, and make a home. The message was loud and clear—I needed to get married and settle down or risk becoming a social outcast and dying alone! Therefore, I set myself the task of finding a husband. Specifically, I pursued a man who had clear expectations about what he wanted from me, a man who would not ask too many questions about my insecurities, and a man who would provide a place for me to take shelter and belong.

Fortunately, the first real candidate that came along was someone who had a common goal in mind. He was a brave, Canadian entrepreneur, a cancer survivor, and the youngest of four in an immigrant family. He was older than I was and had a clear plan of what he wanted his life to look like. His level of certainty and clarity about his path forward—to build his "empire"—was compelling, and I was captivated. He seemed to be a hard worker with good family values. He wanted to be the provider and build a home for us to raise a family in. His plan and expectations were clear, and I felt that I was up to the challenge to meet all of his needs.

Did he adore me? No. Did he value me? No. Did he want to know the real me? No. Somehow, I told myself that these things did not matter. I had myself convinced that marriage was about making my husband happy and that one day, that might make me happy too. I convinced myself that he was good enough and that if I proved my worth, if I met his expectations, and if I gave him everything he wanted, one day, he may even love me too. So, like everything else I did, I jumped in fully to prove myself to him.

What I did not account for was the chaos that would unfold in the years ahead and the personal sacrifice it would require for me to live by his rules and fulfill his expectations. During the course of our 15-year relationship, we navigated a business start-up, a cancer journey, multiple rounds of in-vitro fertilization, raising a busy young family, hostile business takeovers, financial distress, years living in the in-laws' basement, and then, of course, a global health crisis. Though these events are common for many people, the compounding stress levels and build-up of unaddressed trauma, in addition to my own suppressed emotions and personal baggage, eventually took a toll and overcame me.

My hyper-achieving nature had primed me well to tackle all of the adversity that life threw at us in the years of our marriage. We endured one battle after another, and we never spoke about our feelings; we put on a brave face and kept on going. I became so attuned to facing adversity in our marriage that I had completely normalized chaos and suffering. There were no breaks—it was one thing after another. Yes, there were good times and so many things that I remain thankful for, including our three beautiful miracle children. However, over time, the emotional load took a toll on me.

For so long, I had put on the appearance that life was good and everything was fine for the outside world to see, while on the inside, I was in a dark, empty place. It took a lot of energy to manage this diametric existence and keep my inner suffering a secret. Then, after a year into the global health crisis, I couldn't hold up the facade anymore. The lie I had been telling myself and others—that I was happy—came undone. The cracks started to show, and my decades of suppressed emotions started to come to the surface. I had lost myself along the way and then found myself living someone else's life for someone else's sake. This was *his* plan and *his* empire; I was just a player in his game. Though it was what I wanted in the beginning, after 15 years of living this way, I had had enough. The straw that broke the camel's back was my husband's lack of support for my professional ambitions. He wanted me to stay home and care for our home; however, I had a desire to pursue my own entrepreneurial freedom. This was the beginning of the end for us.

Initially, when I launched the company, I simply wanted to use my brain and feel a sense of independence; the flexibility of working for myself rather than an employer seemed appealing because I wanted to be available for my family as much as possible. Then, as I gained traction with a few clients, the business started to grow, and I grew hungry for achievement. Unfortunately, my desire to succeed and emerge as my true self conflicted with my husband's plan for our life. As I rose and gained confidence in myself, he grew increasingly resentful toward me and planted seeds of doubt in the minds of my children about my ability to be a good mom and a successful entrepreneur at the same time. It seemed that the more I owned my truth that I wanted more outside of the home, the more conflict arose between us. It became clear that I was a threat to his plan. It felt that I had a hard decision to make: to choose him or to choose me.

To him, my decision to end the marriage may have come as a shock. I suspect that he did not think I would ever have the courage to stand up to him and break our contract. In truth, it had been something I'd been battling with for some time. Then, as I started to own my truth, his confusion quickly turned into rage. We tried working with a few counselors, but the more questions I answered truthfully in the sessions, the worse things got. At one point, it felt as though there was a plan between the counselor and my husband to convince me to stay and continue to sacrifice myself, but there was something inside of me that said, *No more!* I could not go back to the emotional prison that I had put myself in. I had one chance to realize my freedom, and so I made the hardest decision of my life: I chose me.

Though it was clear that it was necessary for me to leave the marriage in order to save myself, it was not an easy decision, and it came with a lot of painful consequences. I had never put myself first before, and it was unfamiliar and scary. The unfortunate reality was that I had no plan as to what to do next and no support system to turn to for help. I felt lost and alone. What made things even worse still was that I had no idea how ugly he would turn in the separation process and the magnitude of the personal loss that was ahead of me.

The morning after I told my husband that our marriage was over, he sat me and our young family down at the kitchen table and told our children that I was leaving. I cried out in horror and tried to explain to my dear children that this was not the case. I tried to reassure them that I was never going to leave them, but by that stage, the damage was done. From that moment on, my entire world fell out from underneath me.

After losing everything I knew, my home, my family, and my identity, I suddenly had an expansive amount of time alone. The hustle and bustle of my busy family life was replaced with silence. Every moment I spent alone without the noise of children, pets, the stove cooking, or the laundry machine running was deafening and devastating. The silence was so loud that it felt like my eardrums were going to explode inside my head.

In the devastation of my personal life's collapse, I fell hard. The edges of my life were so painfully sharp that there were days I struggled to get up at all. Every morning that I woke up from a restless sleep, I was horrified to find that the nightmare was ever so real. In order to help me cope, I adopted unhealthy vices and numbing behaviors to help me soften the edges of my existence. I drank a lot, stayed in hotels often, shopped irresponsibly, and poured myself into my work for 20 hours a day. Though I tried to hide my pain, shame, and guilt from the outside world, the truth was that I was spiraling fast.

The enormity of the rejection and abandonment hit me hard; everything I feared in my life came true. As I looked around, I found myself completely alone, in a foreign country, without family and support. My parents and brother were back home in Australia in the midst of the health crisis lockdown, so there was no way they could have been with me even if they wanted to. There was no denying it; this was my mess, and it seemed that I was going to have to figure out my way through it. I had gotten myself into this situation, and so I told myself that I had to be the one to get myself out.

As my first Christmas alone approached, a new friend suggested I join her for a Christmas morning clothing drop on the Downtown Eastside in Vancouver. This part of town is known for having the highest population of homeless people and the highest density of drug use in the country. My friend shared that we would be delivering clothes and general supplies to homeless people on the street as a gesture of generosity and kindness that Christmas morning. I was thankful for the escape from my circumstances and the opportunity to be of service to those who needed love and care.

It was freezing on the streets, with subzero temperatures. As we stood out there in the cold with these lost souls, every single one of them was thankful for the clothing and snacks we shared with them. By the end of the day, I was filled with emotion—sensitivity, compassion, relatability, and love— sensations I hadn't felt for a long time. It was a humbling experience because I could see that many people were dealing with much harder things than I was. Somehow, in the mess of my own life, I had something good to offer them, and as it turned out, they also had a lot to teach me.

After talking with so many individuals that day who had lost hope and surrendered to the reality of dying on the streets one day, I felt thankful that I still had a lot of life and possible prosperity ahead of me on the other side of my trauma. Although there was not a lot of hope for change for so many of the people that I had met that day, they helped me see that there was hope for change for me.

As my friend and I started to make our way home, we found a gentleman on the pavement. He looked so peaceful—almost meditative—until we realized that he was not napping—he was unconscious! We stopped, called 911, and stayed on the roadside as the paramedics, fire brigade, and police arrived on site. Fortunately, they were able to revive the man. As they sat him up, everyone went silent when they saw what was written on his shirt. The quote said:

"It's not whether you get knocked down, it's whether you get up."
– Vince Lombardi

As I went home that night to my empty apartment, I couldn't stop thinking about the man we had saved and the people we had spent time with on the street. I felt like I could relate to them because I, too, had been running from my pain. I had abandoned myself. I had lost control of my life. The difference between them and me was that I still had the wherewithal and the capacity to turn my life around. I had the tools, resources, and the intelligence to dig myself out of my circumstances. So why was I holding myself back from embracing the freedom I was seeking?

It was not as though these events had happened to me; after all, I had made the decision to leave my marriage and pursue my freedom. I had decided to stop running from myself and finally own up to who I was and what I wanted. There were no more places to hide, no more excuses to tell myself, and nothing getting in the way of my path to freedom—except me. Once and for all, I had to ask myself, *was I ready to rise?*

CHAPTER 2

THE CLIMB UP

Taking that first step toward reclaiming my identity and rebuilding my life from the ground up was nothing short of terrifying. Facing the path forward alone and unsupported was daunting and overwhelming in every way. What made it even more challenging was that I had forgotten who I really was and lost sight of what I truly wanted—I didn't know where to start.

It felt as though I was sitting at the foothill of a steep mountain climb, unsure of what lay ahead of me along the way and unclear on what awaited me at the top. My low energy levels and lack of strength were concerning. However, I had no alternative plan, so onward I would need to climb.

In order to recreate myself and redesign my life, I would have to confront some hard truths and deal with a lot of what I'd been running from for decades. The reality was that I couldn't run away from myself any longer because there was nowhere left to hide. Part of me believed that there was beauty in the path ahead, and the other part of me was not so sure that I would survive the climb. Without any viable alternatives, because going back to my old life was simply not an option, I surrendered to the fact that there was only one path forward from here—up!

Sure, I had done hard things before, but they had been for the sake and benefit of others. This was unfamiliar territory because I had never put my own needs first or tried to succeed for my own sake. There would be no praise, awards, or recognition from others. All external sources of encouragement that I relied upon to motivate me in the past—were gone. This time, my driving force and motivation were going to have to come from within.

Though I had decided that I was ready to move forward and take this climb up the mountain that lay before me, my mind was getting in the way. My internal dialogue was crippling and disabling me from taking the most basic steps forward. My inner critic became extremely loud, and the self-loathing commentary had me in a spin. Over and over, I heard myself say that I deserved this living hell, that this was my fault, and that I was not worthy of having a good life. All of the past criticism and shaming attacks from my bullies and my husband came flooding in. Often, I agreed with my husband's accusations that I was selfish, unstable, and incapable of doing anything without him. This toxic narrative was paralyzing and quickly became a battlefield of my mind. I would have to find a way to overpower my toxic headspace if I was going to be able to get unstuck and move forward.

During my time living in Whistler, I had befriended several athletes, artists, and entrepreneurs. Their drive and mental toughness were inspirational. Through conversations with them, I started to understand that their success came from the power of their mind first, and their body second. They shared a common mental focus that they practiced daily: the drive to be better today than yesterday. Irrespective of their craft or skills, each of these magnificent beings shared an unrelenting and daily commitment to self-improvement. Their drive came from their positive mindset, which gave them the fuel to commit to doing the hard work every day to climb their personal mountain and pursue their goals.

Through conversations with these extraordinary friends, it became clear that the changes I wanted to make in my life would have to shart with a shift in my mindset. I could not afford for this self-loathing, negative headspace to consume me; I would have to learn how to become mentally stronger to conquer my mind.

One of the books that I used to help shift my mindset was David Goggins' *Can't Hurt Me*. I would listen to the audiobook over and over while running in the forest in the backyard of my home at the base of Whistler Mountain. As David spoke about his personal struggles and mental battles throughout each of the grueling chapters, his words penetrated me deeply. The book helped me to understand that the pain and hardship that I was moving through were part of my mental conditioning process and that I must press on forward. His guidance helped me understand that in the process of building mental toughness, I would have to push through the pain barrier to unlock new levels of my mental and physical potential. It was clear that my mind could be used as my weapon to build strength, or it could become my enemy—I would have to choose.

As I started to dig into my mental barriers and roadblocks more deeply, I explored a range of mindset management approaches. Then, through a conversation with a fellow business coach, I was introduced to the work of Shirzad Chamine, who developed the Positive Intelligence Quotient (PQ) concept. These techniques were proven to help people recognize their negative-centered thinking and shift to a positive mindset. Based on the reading, it seemed that the secret was to weaken the sabotaging thought patterns that come up in the mind with simple and repetitive mind activities that disempower the negative mindset and empower a more positive mindset. The more I examined my thoughts, the more I understood the two primary thought-pattern saboteurs that had been waging war inside my head for decades.

First, there was my inner judge. My inner judge was the ultimate critic who spent every second of every day pointing out all my faults and flaws. My inner judge told me that I was always wrong, that I was a failure, and that I was a fool. Mean right?! Second, the accomplice saboteur was the hyper-achiever. The hyper-achiever mentality had me convinced that nothing I did was ever good enough. It caused me to set extremely high standards for myself and always feel like I was falling short of expectations. With these two saboteurs filling my head with doubt and insecurities, it was no wonder I was a mess!

The more I read, the more I started to appreciate the importance of positive self-talk, and the more I believed that I could take back control of the dialogue in my head and literally change my mind with a shift toward positive thinking. With a combination of trepidation and curiosity, I started to practice positive mindset-shifting practices. What seemed so easy in theory turned out to be a lot harder in practice. Thinking about my thinking was exhausting, but through the application of a handful of techniques, I slowly started to rewrite my code, and it soon started to pay off because I gained confidence in my ability to take positive steps forward on my path.

One Summer morning, while out hiking in the forest again, I received a call from a struggling local entrepreneur who was at risk of losing her business and needed a coach to guide her. Eager to escape my own circumstances for a while and focus my attention on helping someone else out, I said yes to the opportunity. Though, initially, I thought I was going to be doing all of the teaching, as it turned out, I quickly realized that this young entrepreneur was going to show me way more than I could ever teach her.

I still remember every detail of that first call I had with Amy; the fear and fight in her were palpable. She was in a desperate position with her vintage clothing store, which had shut down during the health crisis (like all other businesses at that time) and was at risk of complete financial collapse. She had debt up to her eyeballs, she was going to have to lay off her staff, and she had no idea what she was going to do next to try to save the business.

During one of our working sessions, I asked her why she didn't just shut it all down for good, as many business owners would have. She looked at me, confused. She responded that there was no way she would walk away from the business she had poured her whole self into building. She expressed that the business was her calling in life; she had spent her entire life serving others and working for a range of crappy bosses. When she decided to open the business, it was the first time she had put herself first and followed her heart. She was not prepared to give up on this business because she refused to give up on herself.

Amy had the grit and the conviction she needed to climb the mountain that lay ahead of her; her mindset was positive, she had a solution focus, and she was intent on rising through this period of difficulty. Her head was in the game; all she really needed was some tools and guidance from a business coach to help her solve key issues and take action strategically. Fortunately, I had some relevant business coaching experience and a proven business operating system that could help her restructure her business and rise through the storm she was in, so we got to work tackling one issue at a time.

Slowly but surely, we navigated the path forward to recover Amy's business and restore her financial stability. It was by no means easy; she almost had to shut down her company several times. Despite the challenges, she never gave up on herself, and she never allowed negative thoughts to take control or get in her way. Her determination not only helped her take the necessary steps to keep her business alive, but it also helped her move on and prosper in the years ahead. Amy's mental toughness got her through the most challenging time in her entrepreneurial journey. I learned so much from her in our time working together that I then used it to transform my own mindset and turn around my circumstances.

With practice, I started to build the capacity to control my mindset and shift doubt, fear, and worry into courage and confidence. The daily war in my mind between my positive and negative thoughts was exhausting at times. However, in time, my positive intelligence and inner wisdom won the battle. My efforts were paying off.

As I looked for shortcuts and ways that I could simplify and sustain my mindset practices, I then stumbled across the work of Don Miguel Ruiz in his book called The *Four Agreements*. It was as though he had read my mind. The book features four simple, practical principles for living that can help elevate your positive mindset and quality of life through easy-to-follow personal agreements.

The agreements referenced in the book are:
1. Be impeccable with your words.
2. Don't take anything personally.
3. Don't make assumptions.
4. Always do your best.

Inspired by these agreements, I began developing my own mindset ground rules to help me maintain a positive and empowered state of mind more consistently. These rules helped me to tune my mind and take control of my thoughts and attitudes. Over time, I was able to turn my mind into a tool for positive change rather than a weapon that had previously worked against me. There were days when mindset practice felt ridiculous, and I often resisted it. On many occasions, I strayed from my practice, and my saboteurs got the better of me, causing me to break down and almost give up. However, every time I came back to my rules, I was able to unlock more of the positive power of my mindset. With practice, these rules helped me treat myself with more compassion, understanding, and appreciation for all the hard work I was doing. They also helped me to start to take small steps forward on my healing journey. The mindset rules that I developed to help me take back control of my mind and shift my negative thoughts of doubt and insecurity into positive thoughts of courage and confidence were as follows:

Be Kind, Be Curious, Be Humble, Be Honest, and Be Grateful.

Every morning and throughout the day, I would reflect on these rules and use them to help me choose my mindset. Although so much of my world was changing before me, and so much of it seemed out of my control, it became clear to me that the only thing I could control was my mind.

Practicing these simple mindset rules helped me get unstuck, get out of my own way, and move forward each day. Over time, I was also able to leverage the increasing strength of my mind to go deeper into my inner healing work and eventually build up the capacity to start the journey of redefining and rebuilding my life by my own design.

With a stronger state of mind, I was able to get out of my own way and start to take the early and essential steps forward on my climb up the steep mountain of self-rediscovery and life reconstruction that lay ahead of me. These mindset rules reminded me every day that even though it was hard to see sometimes, I was worthy of the good in my life and all of the good that was yet to come.

In all of the mindset work I have done, I can say that even the smallest of shifts in the mind can make a huge difference over time. It takes hard work and practice, but it does pay off. As I learned to change the way I thought, it then allowed me to change the way I behaved, and then eventually, it helped me to change the outcomes in my life.

The 5 Mindset Rules

For your consideration, I have included a short summary of what each rule has meant to me below. I encourage you to take them as examples that you may like to practice and then, in time, consider adopting your own set of mindset rules.

Be Kind

Kindness is a powerful force that can transform your interactions and relationships. By showing compassion, sensitivity, and understanding, you can bring out the best in yourself and others. Kindness involves being mindful of your thoughts, words, and actions, ensuring they contribute positively to those around you. This also extends to how you treat yourself. Often, we are our harshest critics. By slowing down and observing your thoughts, you can intercept negative, self-sabotaging narratives and adopt a wiser, more compassionate approach. This leads to a healthier relationship with yourself and more intentional and impactful relationships with others.

Be Honest

Honesty is about taking responsibility for your thoughts and words. It means acting with integrity in all your interactions. By bravely confronting the truth and addressing real issues with brutal honesty, you can remove barriers to happiness and fulfillment. Change begins with acknowledging what is and is not working in your life. Honesty with yourself is crucial for self-growth, and honesty with others reduces complexity and confusion. Saying what you mean and meaning what you say saves time and energy, building deeper trust and connections with those around you.

Be Curious

Curiosity opens the door to deeper understanding and compassion. By releasing judgment and embracing curiosity, you can better understand the perspectives and behaviors of others. Avoiding assumptions removes barriers to connection and fosters empathy. When you explore your own perceptions of reality, you gain insight into the stories you tell yourself and why you think and act the way you do. During times of frustration or resistance, curiosity can help you tackle the underlying issues and find solutions that lead to personal growth and improved relationships.

Be Grateful

Gratitude shifts your focus away from what is lacking in your life and instead toward what is present and available to appreciate. Being able to recognize the gifts in your life will help you stay thankful even when times are tough. Gratitude helps you to see the value in every experience, including hardship, and encourages an attitude of perseverance and resilience throughout daily life. This positive outlook can help you to build confidence and elevate your quality of life with a simple shift in thinking.

Be Humble

Humility involves recognizing that all humans are imperfect and designed to struggle. Embracing your imperfections and vulnerability creates openness and space for learning and growth. Showing humility in your relationships removes judgment and unrealistic expectations, making you more approachable and fostering deeper relationships. Humility allows you to see the humanity in others, enhancing your ability to connect with others. Reframing personal failures through the lens of humility can help unlock learning and development even when things don't work out as planned.

Coaching Guidance

If you want to make positive changes in your life but feel stuck in your mindset battlefield, please know that you are not alone. Everyone struggles with their saboteurs and can get caught in a place of indecision and inaction. Though you might have the desire to create meaningful, positive changes in your life, the reality is that your mind will continue to be your greatest obstacle until you learn to control and conquer it.

As you will have heard me mention already, you and I are the main characters in all of the challenges in our lives. Though we may want the world to change for us, the truth is that it won't, but you and I can. In reality, we don't control anything other than our minds, and when we change the way we think, we change the way we behave, and then we change the results we get.

Real change starts with the mind.

Here is a quick exercise that can help to create some positive shifts and increase your confidence to take on the battle of your mind. ***This exercise is also featured in the free companion guide, which is accessible via the QR code included in this book.***

Changing Your Mindset Exercise

1. Make a list of the two or three primary negative thoughts that consistently show up in your mind and hold you back from taking positive action to make the changes you want to see in your life.

_____

_____

_____

2. List two positive counter statements that show wisdom and affirm yourself as a good, capable, and worthy human. If you struggle here, think of the language you would use if a good friend expressed that they were struggling with the same saboteur in part one. Be as specific as you can.

_____

_____

_____

3. Review the positive thought statements and distill the list down to one positive, affirming statement that you feel will help you interrupt your internal negative narrative and create a positive shift in your mindset.

_____

_____

_____

4. Write out your affirmation statement on a post-it note and place it somewhere that you will see it daily, such as on your bedside table or your laptop keypad. Reference it daily and notice the shift in mindset and mood that takes place.

_____

_____

_____

Example:

Negative Statement: "I can't do anything right. I am a failure." This statement held me back from taking risks and making changes because I was too afraid to fail.

Positive Statement: "In between my expectations and outcomes, there is space for growth. Even when I feel like I am failing, the truth is that I am learning." This new mindset gives me the courage to make changes and take risks, as I now understand that even if I fail, I learn and improve.

CHAPTER 3

BREAKING THE PATTERN

With my willingness to give myself a chance to succeed and the commitment to keep my mindset rules in practice every day, I bravely started my journey up the mountain to reclaim myself and rebuild my life. The first steps out of the ruins of my personal life were by no means easy because I did not know who I really was, and I did not know what I truly wanted in my life. Though I wanted to take a break and make the time to contemplate the possibilities ahead of me, the reality of my circumstances compelled me to take action quickly; there was no time to delay action. I had a legal battle on my hands, a business that I had to keep running in order to pay my bills, and I needed to find a place to call home so that I could spend time with my children to the extent that they would allow it.

In the later stages of our difficult marriage and during the global health crisis, I moved to live in Whistler with our children while my husband worked in the city and took care of his parents. He would come up on weekends to spend time with us and then head down to work every Monday morning. We were like many other families who made the move out of the city during that time because the pandemic was taking hold of the city, and it seemed to make sense to get out of town to be close to nature and wait out the chaos.

During that time, Whistler became my safe haven and a reprieve from the turbulence of our busy city life and our rocky marriage. Before long, I had immersed myself and my children in the community there. In so many ways, the forest and the mountains provided a sense of security and strength at a time when I needed it most. The unhealthy state of our marriage was taking a toll on me, and I was starting to crack under the pressure. This break from our hectic city life was a welcomed break for me. It gave me space to think and room to breathe. Interestingly, the more time I spent away from my husband, the healthier I felt. When he was away in the city working, I felt my nervous system relax, and I slept better than ever. In time, I realized that I was not broken—the marriage was.

Sadly, when the marriage ended, it triggered a landslide that pulled my family and home from my grasp, leaving me completely alone and displaced. On a regular Friday transition, I dropped my children off at school, trusting that they would be picked up and returned by their dad the following Monday. However, all of a sudden, only one of the three came home. I remember the terror that shot through my body. I fought and protested the decision, but it fell on deaf ears—my children were gone, and they were not coming home. The impact on my being remains indescribable. It felt as though my inner core collapsed inside of me.

As if the alienation of my children had not been bad enough, in an act of cruelty, I then received notice that he would be making a court application to have me removed from our Whistler vacation home. It seemed inhumane and impossible that the court would prove it, but sadly, the judge approved his application, and, in that moment, I became homeless.

Though my displacement as a mother and homelessness shook me to the core, unlike in the past, I was determined not to let him take me down. My mindset rules helped me to stay steady, keep my mind in a positive space, and take action quickly. I jumped into my research and, humbled, asked for help from people in the Whistler community to find a rental space. I was willing to take a spare room if I had to. With a forward-focused attitude, I soon found a suite through a new friend and settled myself into a little A-frame cabin at the foot of the mountain. If not for my mindset rules to help me, I would have likely sat in my mess for a longer period of time and potentially missed out on the opportunity to take control of my circumstances and achieve such a great result.

Change was in motion whether I liked it or not. Every day, I was being called to make decisions and advocate for myself, which was an unfamiliar concept because I had been living for the sake of others for so long. My challenge wasn't so much a lack of opportunities, but rather the overwhelming possibilities and the high stakes of making a poor decision. In truth, I didn't yet trust myself to make good decisions and protect my own interests; this was all so new to me. As I tackled one issue at a time and made every effort to move forward, I had a lingering fear that I might fall back into my old patterns of self-sacrificing and self-sabotaging if I was not careful. I couldn't afford to go back; I had to move forward, and I had to break my old patterns. It was clear that I needed to break this pattern of the past. However, I knew that it was not going to be easy and I would need some professional support.

Therapy seemed like a good place to start. One of the first therapists I worked with was particularly helpful in supporting me to understand my pattern. Not only were we able to name the issue, but we were also able to identify the root cause of childhood events that triggered the decades of problems that followed. This therapist also helped me to recognize that I was not alone. All people pick up stories and patterns along their journey. It was a relief to hear that I was not the only one. If you have ever done deep inner work, you can attest to the fact that it is both messy and necessary. In order to understand our patterns, we need to travel backward through the hardships of life and find that moment when a difficult experience caused us to form a narrative about life and a behavioral pattern designed to protect ourselves from that hardship in the future. The unfortunate thing is that the story and the pattern that is then triggered typically do not serve us well long term, and that is where the trouble starts.

As I started working backward through my difficult journey in search of that triggering event, I started to see some themes and patterns emerge that presented me with some hard truths. It became clear that I was the common theme, the main character in my difficult life events; it seemed that I was the common problem every time.

Along the journey backward into my past, I observed a series of outstanding achievements that I had made in an effort to be approved by my teachers, coaches, parents, bosses, and so on. Then, with each peak, a hard fall would follow shortly after. Each of the falls was caused by burnout and triggered a nasty thread of self-loathing criticism that would result in deep shame, regret, humiliation, and fear. Over the years, these events caused an accumulation of emotional baggage that went unaddressed and covered up as I ran toward the next challenge in front of me.

As I looked back at these events, I asked myself: *Why was I trying so hard to please others? Why did I feel that I wasn't enough?* Every time I met the needs or expectations of others and pleased them, I enjoyed it and experienced a shot of dopamine, but I never felt satisfied. There were times that I was convinced that something was wrong with me because I did not feel anything positive at all. While others seemed happy with the outcomes, I felt empty. *Why did I keep trying if I kept coming up empty in my people-pleasing ways? What did I really want?* I needed to find out.

Prior to my marriage, my need to please others had caused me to pursue a top-tier job at one of the world's largest accounting firms in an effort to make my parents proud. I was ambitious and hungry to prove to my parents that they raised me well and to give them a payoff for all they had done for me. I earned my seat at the table with a first-class organization, but that was not enough for me. I put my hand up for every opportunity to make an impact, and I took on extra assignments in an effort to be approved by the firm's leadership. In just two years, I moved roles three times, seeking bigger challenges with each change. After running this people-pleasing and overachieving cycle for too long, I finally ran out of gas and crashed. I was burnt out; I had lost my way inside the enormous organization, and I felt that

I had no option but to leave out of humiliation and desperation to escape the situation I'd put myself in.

Working back further into my youth, I saw the same unhealthy patterns of behavior show up in my high school years. All throughout my schooling, I had an unrelenting desire to please my teachers and make my parents proud. The need for approval and acceptance resulted in top grades year after year, a long list of leadership achievements, and the award of the Head Student position in grade twelve. Once again, I had gone too far and overextended myself. Then, during my final exams, I cracked under the pressure, had a major mental breakdown, and barely finished the year out. The pressure I'd put myself under was too much; I broke and fell hard.

All along the way, I had been repeating the same unhealthy pattern without even realizing it. I would seek an opportunity to please or impress people I looked up to; I would push too hard and crack under the pressure I had placed upon myself. No one else had said I needed to reach that high; neither my parents nor my teachers ever set those expectations for me—I was doing it to myself. Sadly, when I would push too hard, I would consistently crack under the pressure and run away in shame. *Where was this need to please coming from?*

The therapist challenged me and urged me to go back deeper into my childhood to search for the source of this nasty pattern. It wasn't easy, and I did not want to do it, but there was no way around this—it had to be done.

This search led me back to my primary school years. From the age of five, I struggled to fit in with my classmates. I was overweight, awkward, and never seemed to find my way into circles of acceptance. I was aware of my differences and became deeply fearful of being left out. I wanted so desperately to be liked. Back then, there were pecking orders for everything. When sports teams were created, the best athletes were chosen as the captains, and they would then stand up at the front of the class and select the kids they wanted to have on their team. I never made it to the preferred list—I was always among the leftover options once the best had been chosen. Additionally, clubs were very popular when I was young; there was a club for every hobby and interest group under the sun. But, I never seemed to make it into any of the clubs that I wanted to be part of.

I always felt like I was on the outer edge, and before long, my differences made me a prime target for bullies. From the first year of school and every year thereafter, I was bullied relentlessly. In response to my struggles with my classmates and in the search for belonging, I turned my attention to the teachers and became the "Teacher's Pet." This certainly did not go over well with the bullies on the playground, and I soon became their number one target.

The more I grew to be favored by my teachers, the worse the bullying became. It then carried on for all of my elementary school years and became a normal part of my school experience. I was verbally attacked, pushed around, hit often, and regularly chastised in front of groups of children on the playground.

Though difficult, it did not seem serious enough to bring to the attention of my teachers, so I endured the mistreatment in silence. I thought I could manage it on my own, but then, one rainy day during lunch hour, things got out of control.

All the kids were inside for the play break, and everything was fine until word hit the rumor mill that Shane, my primary bully, had reached his limit of disgust with me and decided that he wanted to teach me a lesson. He spread a rumor that he had a knife in his bag and was going to kill me after school. Instantly, the news made its way to me.

It hit me like a ton of bricks; I hadn't prepared for this level of threat. Sure, the bullying had been unpleasant and difficult in the past, but it had never reached this level. This death threat presented a life-or-death situation, something I could never even have imagined. I went into a state of panic. Terror shot through my body, and I freaked out. I ran through the hallway, searching for a teacher to help me. I didn't feel safe in my own body—my chest was bursting, I could taste metal in my mouth, and my entire being was vibrating. I finally found the vice-principal and did my best to explain what was happening while in the middle of a panic attack. They said they would take it from there and sent me off to the nurse's room to wait it out.

As I sat there, I remember contemplating death for the first time in my life; it was scary and overwhelming. Images of murder scenes from movies I had watched in the past came flooding in. *Was this really going to happen to me? What did the funeral of an 11-year-old look like? How would my parents feel if I died?* It felt like an endless period of waiting before one of the male teachers came to collect me. He then walked me over to a classroom where Shane sat waiting. Just looking at him sent me into shock, and I shut down internally; it was too much for me to handle. I sat there in silence, desperate to get my breathing under control to avoid passing out.

As I looked toward the door, I noticed the little heads of my classmates peeking in from the hallway to see what was going on; I felt mortified. Fortunately, I didn't have to say much, and the teacher tore strips off Shane. He forced him to apologize, and Shane was put on weeks of much-deserved detention. Despite the matter being dealt with by everyone else's standards, it was far from over for me. The damage was done. From this experience, I told myself that it was not safe for me to be different because it could get me killed. That day, my innocent "child-self" went into hiding, and my "people-pleasing protector" persona was born; the play stopped, and the work began. It then became my mission to please and seek shelter in the protection of anyone who made me feel safe. At each stage of my life thereafter, I would quickly assess who was in power and make it my mission to please them, to earn their favor, and to stay safe—at all costs.

Revealing the root cause of my pattern was not only eye-opening but also overwhelming. I was just a child who wanted to fit in, have friends, and play. These events, as well as the patterns I developed as a result, caused me to abandon my inner child because it was not safe. Rather than playing and having fun, I hid myself away and put my energy into managing risk, staying small, and pleasing others in an effort to stay out of harm's way. As I sat processing these hard truths, waves of emotion overcame me.

Deep sadness, regret, and disappointment washed over me, but then came compassion and forgiveness toward myself for all that I had been through. The last person that I had surrendered my power to was my husband, and I could see now that I dedicated myself to him and poured myself into pleasing him in an effort to stay safe. With no one left to please and serve, I found myself at yet another critical decision point: *Was I ready to break the cycle and come out of hiding as my true self?*

At long last, I decided it was time to break the pattern of being who I thought I needed to be for the sake of others, and finally become my true and fully empowered self, and learn how to be secure in my own skin. There could be no more running into the arms of a man or an authority figure in search of love and security. There could be no more outsourcing my validation and worth to the hands of others. It was time to come out of hiding and learn a new way of living by myself—for myself.

Forming this commitment to change my story and break my pattern proved to be a significant milestone on my transformation journey. It gave me a new sense of commitment to myself to move forward toward my life of independence and greater confidence in my ability to pursue my next chapter in life on my own.

Coaching Guidance

Understanding our personal patterns is challenging work. If you are looking at taking this journey inward to unpack your patterns and seek to make changes in your life, I recommend engaging in professional support and being patient with yourself. Remember, you have spent decades living in this cycle, so it can take some time to create the changes you want to see in your life.

In the following pages, I have included a short exercise that outlines one of the techniques that I used to help me trace my lifeline back to understand my pattern and its source. ***This exercise is also featured in the free companion guide accessible via the QR code featured in this book. In it, you will have the space to capture your notes.***

Disclaimer: this exercise is a discovery process, not an aimless reason to torture yourself or a pointless reason to re-live your past pain all over again. The goal here is to create breakthroughs in your understanding of your patterns. If you give yourself the opportunity to understand your patterns and get to their root cause, there is a chance that you will then be able to regain control of the story and make significant positive changes in your life. Although you may feel that these events happened *to you*, it is also possible that these events happened *for you* to inspire learning and personal transformation.

My hope is that through this process, you will appreciate the fact that although you can't go back to changing the past, you can definitely change your future by breaking the patterns that no longer serve your best interests. It's never too late for change. When you are ready to let go of past behaviors that no longer benefit you, I am confident that you will unlock positive forward momentum on your healing and transformation journey.

Breaking Your Pattern Exercise

1. Chart your life backward and identify three key events that shaped you. These defining moments will be experiences that shaped your view of yourself in relation to the rest of the world. Name them and write them down.

_____

_____

_____

2. Keep going back through your childhood until you reach the most difficult experiences that you are uncomfortable thinking and talking about. Identify the earliest and most difficult life event and name the life lesson it taught you.

_____

_____

_____

3. As you reflect on these experiences, describe the story you told yourself about life in response to these events. Identify the narratives and write them down.

_____

_____

_____

4. Do your best to connect the story you told yourself with the behavioral adaptations that you implemented in response to your hardship and narrative. Identify the behaviors and write them down.

_____

_____

_____

5. Identify the ways that this behavioral pattern has helped and hindered you on your personal journey. Be as specific as you can.

_____

_____

_____

6. Develop a wise alternative narrative to counteract the story that you told yourself.

_____

_____

_____

7. Form a commitment toward making a behavior change to help you to break your pattern of behavior.

_____

_____

_____

CHAPTER 4

BUILDING ENERGY

It was time to come out of hiding, break my old patterns, and once and for all take control of my life. Intellectually, I understood what needed to be done in order to take charge of my circumstances, and I was emotionally committed to doing the work to take this brave step forward toward my independence for the first time in my life. The challenge was that my energy level was extraordinarily low. I barely had enough fuel in my energy tank to get out of bed and face the day, let alone take charge of my life and my destiny. I felt stuck in my energy trap and doubtful about whether I could build up enough reserves to make it up the climb ahead of me.

Without external support, I needed to find a way to build up my own strength and create more energy capacity so that I could start the process of rebuilding my life. How could I do that when I could barely make it through the workday without falling asleep on my laptop? I had my business to run so that I could pay my bills, and I had my youngest child with me half the time, who needed my love, care, and attention. It felt like there was nothing left at the end of the day for me. Taking time off or going to a healing retreat was not an option; I had no time and resources for that. I would have to find a way to build up my energy capacity while simultaneously running on the low battery I had.

Fortunately, my unrelenting brain likes to solve complex problems, and so I set myself the challenge of figuring out how to build up my energy levels. This led me down the path to better understanding the mechanics of human energy and finding strategies to help me manage my own energy more effectively. I read countless books and listened to a range of podcasts on the topic of personal development and energy management. The more I researched the subject, the more I wanted to know.

Then, one day, I made an important realization. I discovered that I already had years of teaching and coaching energy management as an entrepreneurial business coach. The key skill I had been teaching leaders was to manage their primary resources in their business—human energy. With simple tools and disciplines, I would help these entrepreneurial leaders improve their level of accountability and disciplined execution so that they could then, as a result, elevate the capacity of their teams and take the business to the next level.

My passion for helping improve the capacity and performance of entrepreneurial businesses came about from my own experience of helping to turn around the technology business that my husband and I owned. From the day I arrived in Canada and through ten years of marriage, the business consumed us completely. Day after day, it felt as though the business owned us rather than the other way around, and no matter how hard we worked, it did not get any better. I was convinced that there had to be a better way to run the company and that it should not be this hard. Yet, I quickly found that no matter how hard we tried to make changes, the same recurring issues came up time and time again. We found it difficult to hire and retain good people; we struggled to keep up with demand; we experienced internal battles between departments, and our costs spiraled out of control. The business had hit a ceiling. We were stuck and at a loss as to what to do next.

My family back home in Australia could see that we were struggling. In an effort to help us get out of our funk, my brother introduced me to a book and a business operating system model that he was using with his own company. After a quick read of the book *Traction* by Gino Wickman, which entailed the details of the system, it seemed possible that this seemingly simple and practical methodology could have the potential to help us get unstuck. After reading the book, I could clearly see that our business had hit the ceiling, and the method seemed to have the guidance within it to help us hire better and improve the level of accountability across the business so that we could gain control and take the business to the next level. With nothing better available, it seemed worthwhile to at least give it a try.

I appointed myself as the project manager of the implementation process and went to work changing the way we ran the business. Although the team pushed back on the changes initially, over time, they started to adopt the tools and disciplines because they could see how the habits made their work easier and improved the level of collaboration across the company. The simple tools and disciplines featured in the book helped us to create a clear company vision that the team could align with; they helped us to increase the level of daily discipline and accountability, and they helped us to improve the overall communication and team health across the business. For the first time in our entrepreneurial journey, we felt in control of the business and better able to manage all of the human energy in the company.

Through my first-hand experience of helping to turn around our own small business, I then discovered my calling to help other business owners increase the performance potential of their business with this proven framework. With the desire to help many more business owners unlock the human potential of their business and get to the next level, I became an EOS Implementer® in 2018 and launched my business coaching practice. The work was so rewarding because it allowed me to help entrepreneurial leadership teams implement practical tools and disciplines so that they could gain control of the company, unlock the human potential of the business, grow confidently, and take their business to the next level.

Looking back on my professional journey as an EOS Implementer®, I began to explore the possibility of drawing from everything I had learned in business optimization coaching and taking a similar approach to help me manage my own energy and rise above my circumstances. All of the personal development materials I read and listened to also pointed to the proven power of habit to help people manage their energy, elevate their performance, and realize positive changes in their lives. The struggle I was having was that I was overwhelmed by all of the suggestions; I didn't know where to start. With my business optimization methods in mind, it seemed that if I kept it simple with a small number of disciplines and practiced them often, I might be able to get out of my funk and gain control of the one thing I was struggling with most — managing my energy.

So I went to work and put myself to the test to try a range of suggested habits and techniques to see what worked and what did not work for me. My yardstick was that if it increased my energy level and confidence, then it was worth continuing; if it frustrated or depleted me, then I would discard it. Some of the techniques I played with helped, and others didn't. I practiced a lot of grounding techniques, including journaling, meditation, and gratitude walks. Some of the physical activities that I tried included yoga, cycling, and hiking. I also explored a range of restorative methods, such as reflexology, massage, and breathwork. With each of these modalities, I experienced positive results; however, for the most part, I found it difficult to integrate them into my week and maintain them over time. It seemed that I may be trying to do too much at once.

As a child, I heard a lot about my father's upbringing—he was raised on a dairy farm and attended a small, rural school. As the only boy in the family, he was solely responsible for helping his dad run the farm. In addition to his daily chores, which started at 4:00 a.m. and included feeding the cows, cleaning the stalls, and milking the cows, he also had to walk himself to school for several miles each day. Although his childhood was challenging, my dad acknowledged that it taught him the power of discipline, routine, and daily habits. This disciplined and ritualistic way of living was something he carried forward into his adult life.

Throughout my childhood, I watched him maintain his simple and consistent daily routine: he woke up at the same time, did the same morning routine, went to work on schedule, then returned home for dinner at the same time and ended the day exactly the same way with a dessert, tv and then bed. Day after day, he was able to find the energy to provide for our family, be a loving parent, volunteer in our community, and maintain our home with a steady hand and a lot of composure. It seemed that his daily routine and habits were the source of his strength and endurance. They provided the energy he needed to thrive professionally, to provide for our family, and to be both a great husband and a great father.

Over the years, my dad tried to impart to my brother and me the power of daily habits. He would challenge us to exercise daily, practice our sports often, study hard every night, and always plan for the day ahead. As the typical teenager that I was at the time, I would often protest or push back simply because I didn't want to do what I was told, but upon reflection, he had a point. As I reflected on the childhood lessons from my dad, a light bulb came on inside of me. Rather than trying to make big changes to my behavior, I decided I would be better off focusing my efforts on a small number of daily rituals to help me increase my capacity and build up my energy reserves. I did not need to work harder; I needed to do less, get smarter, and harness the power of simple daily habits.

Reading the book *Atomic Habits* by James Clear was a timely reminder for me about the importance of taking a simplified approach to habit development. The content of the book helped me to confirm that it was indeed best to start with small atomic-level behavioral shifts in order to help me build up the capacity for habit development and sustain the behaviors over time. James Clear demonstrated that many people struggled to make positive behavioral changes in their lives because they would try to do too much too quickly and fail. One of the examples I loved most in the book was the reference to building a habit of going to the gym. Rather than setting the bar too high with a goal to go to the gym every day for multiple hours, he would suggest working up to that level by starting with atomic-level habits such as packing your runners in a gym bag and putting them in your car, even if you don't use them, it is still a form of progress.

The book also helped me to understand that I was struggling to make progress with my habit development journey because I had set the bar too high, yet again, and lacked focus on what was most important for me to start with. With the desire to be more intentional with my energy and to keep my practice simple, I chose to focus on one thing—my morning routine. At my lowest point, I was struggling to get up in the morning and face the day. The horror of waking up to my living nightmare was overwhelming, and I would often lay in bed fighting with myself about whether I should get up at all. Some days, I would lie there for three hours stuck in this dilemma and almost give up the fight; however, eventually, I would muster up the courage to give the day a chance and get up. This seemed like a good place to start to make changes because I was losing too much time each morning, and I needed a more efficient routine to get me out of bed and put me in a good frame of mind to start my day.

Rather than trying to implement a perfect morning ritual, I decided that it would make more sense to start working with a simpler approach with some journaling and breathwork to help me reduce the 3-hour morning grind by 5 minutes a day. With a realistic plan in place and a reasonable goal to attain, over time, I slowly brought my morning ritual down to 30 minutes and then eventually 15 minutes a day. To help me stay on task, I would write down my top priorities for the day, choose and name my mindset approach, and make a positive affirmation statement for myself to help remind me that I was a good person. This morning habit gave me a quiet space for introspection, allowing me to focus my mind on what was most important and giving me the opportunity to start the day with a prioritized action plan in place. The more I practiced it, the easier it got for me to get up and get going efficiently. Even to this day, I continue to practice my morning daily stillness ritual; I could not imagine starting the day without it.

This daily stillness ritual became the starting point from which I began to establish a handful of additional healthy day-to-day habits. In each case, I continued to ensure that I kept it simple, made it easy, and took it one day at a time. Eventually, I established five practical habits that helped me to incrementally increase my energy capacity levels over time. I named these habits:

Daily Stillness, Solution Focus, Plan Ahead, See Progress, and Playtime.

Putting each of them into practice was not easy at first. In fact, the habit of playtime was one of the hardest to establish because I had fallen out of practice in experiencing any level of joy and fun in my life. It took some time to figure out what fun could look like for me and a lot of trial and error to find out what felt good. I started with simple things such as carrying around tennis gear in the back of my car with the hope that I might one day try it and enjoy it. One friend asked me if I played tennis, and I replied, "No," and explained that I was in the process of learning how to have fun and tennis seemed like something worth trying out one day soon. They laughed and then offered to teach me how to play.

Though uncomfortable, I kept coming back to the practice of learning how to be playful each day and eventually discovered that I enjoyed doing a range of things for fun rather than purpose or service. Some of the things I found that I truly loved to do were hiking, vintage shopping, and visiting the local farmers market on Saturdays. Before long, I was integrating play into my daily life and felt great about it.

With practice and consistency, my work on these habits started to pay off. I felt increasingly energized, I was able to achieve more each day, and my confidence levels reached an all-time high. Additionally, I felt sure that if I remained committed to my practice, I would be able to pursue the climb ahead of me to rebuild my life for my own sake.

Coaching Guidance

Establishing healthy habits can be difficult and challenging for all of us, but the payoff is high. Habits allow us to build energy levels and increase our capacity over time, empowering us to then take action to upgrade our lives. If you're interested in learning more about my daily habit practices and how some of them may help you improve your ability to elevate your energy and build capacity to embrace your life to the fullest extent, I have included them below and also *referenced them in the free companion guide and mini-course accompanying this book.*

Daily Stillness Habit

What It Is: Daily stillness involves dedicating a portion of your morning to sitting quietly and centering yourself. This practice, which can range from five to thirty minutes, involves slowing down to come into your body, allowing yourself to observe your thoughts without judgment, and setting positive intentions for the day. This habit can help ground you, reduce stress, and enhance your focus, providing a foundation of calm and clarity to begin each day.

How to Implement:

1. **Choose a quiet spot:** Find a peaceful place where you won't be disturbed.
2. **Focus on your breath:** Pay attention to your breathing to help quiet your mind.
3. **Observe your thoughts:** Witness your thoughts roll in and, one by one, release them.
4. **Set your intentions:** Identify your highest priorities for the day and write them down.

Benefits:

- This habit can help you to increase your self-awareness and mindfulness, allow you to prioritize your personal needs, and start each day in a calmer and more intentional way.

Solution Focus Habit

What It Is: Solution focus is a mindset practice of shifting your attention from dwelling on problems to actively seeking solutions. This habit involves recognizing challenges as they arise and quickly identifying actionable steps to address them. Inspired by Dr. Jason Selk's *Relentless Solution Focus*, this approach emphasizes the importance of focusing on what you can control, shifting from problem-centered thinking to solution focus, and taking proactive steps to change your outcomes.

How to Implement:

1. **Notice your thoughts:** Notice when your thoughts are circling on a problem.
2. **Identify the problem:** Name the root of the issue quickly.
3. **Shift your focus:** Ask yourself what you can do to shift your circumstances.
4. **Identify a solution:** Name the course of action you intend to take to solve the problem.
5. **Take positive action:** Implement the steps you've identified and observe the outcomes.

Benefits:

- This habit can help you to reduce negative thinking, improve your proactive problem-solving skills, elevate your clarity and confidence, and help you take action quickly.

Plan Ahead Habit

What It Is: Planning ahead involves looking forward to the day or week ahead and ensuring that you prioritize what matters most to you. This proactive approach ensures you manage your time and energy efficiently. Drawing inspiration from Steven R. Covey's *The 7 Habits of Highly Effective People*, this habit emphasizes the importance of beginning with the end in mind, helping you rise above the chaos in order to focus on what truly matters and move toward desired outcomes with confidence.

How to Implement:

1. **Make the time:** Set aside time each week to plan your 7-day outlook.
2. **Set priorities:** Identify your top three actions for the week that work toward your goals.
3. **Set intentions:** Identify actions to elevate health, fuel growth, and improve relationships.
4. **Integrate daily:** Review the weekly plan while doing daily stillness to stay on track.

Benefits:

- This habit helps to shift your behavior from a reactive state to a proactive state, improve time management capabilities, and can help you focus on achieving meaningful outcomes that matter to you.

See Progress Habit

What It Is: Seeing progress involves regularly reflecting on your achievements and recognizing your growth. This habit shifts your mindset from focusing on shortcomings to celebrating successes. Inspired by Dan Sullivan and Dr. Benjamin Hardy's *The Gap and the Gain*, this practice encourages you to focus on the gains you've made rather than the gap or shortfall between where you are and where you want to be. This will help to inspire and maintain forward momentum toward your goals.

How to Implement:

1. **Evening reflection:** Spend a few minutes each evening looking back on the day to recognize outcomes and progress.
2. **Weekly reflection:** Sit at the end of the week to identify the wins and progress made toward your goals and well-being.
3. **90-day reflection:** Take the time to acknowledge your achievements for the quarter and recognize your goal accomplishments.

Benefits:

This habit helps to encourage a positive mindset, can reinforce progress made and achievements, and can motivate continued effort toward personal growth and goals.

Playtime Habit

What It Is: Playtime is about creating space for happiness and pleasure in your life. Engaging in activities that bring you joy and allow you to unwind is crucial for your overall well-being. This habit, inspired by the need for balance, as highlighted in various wellness practices, encourages you to reconnect with your inner child and make time for playful activities.

How to Implement:

1. **Identify fun things:** Name activities that you would find pleasurable if you had time.
2. **Schedule playtime:** Book time in your weekly schedule for a small number of these activities.
3. **Be spontaneous:** As new invitations come up during the week, say "yes" more.

4. **Unplug:** When taking breaks from work, fully disconnect to enjoy playtime with presence.

Benefits:
- This habit can help to bring more joy and enrichment to your life, can help improve work and life balance, and encourages creativity and adventure to enhance life fulfillment.

CHAPTER 5

START WITH FOCUS

Although it was challenging at first to shift my behavior and adopt new habits, over time, I noticed that the more I practiced the habits, the easier they became and the more they started to integrate into my regular days and weeks with more consistency. What was even more rewarding was to see that these simple habits started to help me increase my energy level, improve my mental clarity, and elevate my overall confidence. With this improved energy capacity, I felt I had the courage and strength to start the climb to rebuild my life, one steady foot in front of the other.

This growing confidence in my ability to move forward in my life gave me the courage to lift my gaze from staring down at my feet and start looking up at the possibilities that lay ahead of me. The more I looked up, the more possibilities I could see ahead of me, and soon, I became overwhelmed by all of the new pathways and opportunities in front of me. It felt surreal to move so quickly from feeling like I had nothing to live for, to now an abundance of life possibilities. I could change my profession, I could change my friends, I could live wherever I wanted, I could change my appearance and much more. One thing was clear: this was my path, and these were my choices.

Whether I succeeded or failed, whether I found happiness or hardship, was completely up to me. Though my mindset was improving and my energy levels were increasing, I still had many unanswered questions about who I really was, what I truly wanted, and where I wanted to go, and I would need to figure this out before I made any drastic moves or big decisions.

In the past, I had been a people-pleasing, "yes" person who lived in service of others every day. My lack of self-confidence and acceptance caused me to avoid my own inner search for meaning and connection, and instead, I poured my energy into meeting the needs of others. Every day, I chased acceptance, validation, and acknowledgment to fill my own inner void. This caused me to say yes to every request for help. I would race to the aid of others, and I always sought out opportunities to make people happy. I would never really stop to think about it. I would just jump all the way in. at the chance to save anyone from a tough situation. After decades of living this way, I had normalized a constant obsession to serve others; the need to be needed was overwhelming. Through this unhealthy pattern of behavior, I gained some friends. However, I lost more than I gained because I would often take things a little too far and get myself into trouble.

While on a family vacation with our children and my husband's friends, my need to help others got the better of me and caused hardship to my own family. It was supposed to be a warm and enjoyable Summer vacation, but then the weather turned cold, and so did the mood. On the second night I received a distressing call from the girlfriend of my husband's long-time friend. She was crying uncontrollably and shared that there had been a major argument after her boyfriend had been drinking and had become abusive. She had packed her suitcase and begged me to save her from her situation. Without even thinking, I jumped into my car and drove to her rescue.

Over the course of the next two days, I cared for her emotionally and physically. I made soup and coaxed her to stay hydrated. When she felt strong enough, I then drove her back into the city, helped her break into the boyfriend's house to collect her belongings, and settled her safely back into her own condo in downtown Vancouver. For weeks afterward, I dealt with the backlash from my husband and the ridicule from his circle of friends. What made it worse was that she went back to her abusive boyfriend within weeks!

As I thought about all of the doors of possibility and unlimited options on my path ahead, one thing was clear: I needed to resist the temptation to put others' needs above my own; this time, I had to take action for my own sake. In order to move forward on my own path, I would have to avoid becoming distracted by help from others, and I would need to become intentional about where I put my energy and set boundaries to avoid defaulting to my old ways.

This inner battle with myself was compounded by the fact that I was struggling with my worthiness after having broken apart my marriage and my family. I was deeply aware of the hardship I had caused everyone and felt the weight of that burden bear down on me every day. Additionally, the sudden loss of my family was nothing short of devastating; I felt unwanted and like a complete failure. As I sat with this enormous void in my life, I felt a yearning to be wanted and needed. In that moment, I had to make the decision whether to default to filling my life with people who needed me or to take action for myself this time. Fortunately, I chose *me*. Building the courage to say no to others and practicing putting myself first was uncomfortable initially, but over time, I noticed that people actually started to respect me for it, and this practice allowed me to buy back time for my own healing journey.

Some of the small changes that I started to make included saying no to Zoom calls, declining coffee dates, and not making time for random people anymore. The more I protected my time and energy, the more it helped me to make progress on my own personal re-creation journey. Yes, I missed the dopamine kick I got from pleasing others, but it was soon replaced by a different sensation, a deeper sense of satisfaction from putting my own needs first. To help me stay on task, prioritize my needs above all else, and avoid distractions, I started to write down my commitments to myself and my intentions at the beginning of each day as part of my morning daily stillness. Rather than worrying about all of the things on my never-ending to-do list or trying to tackle big projects on any given day, I decided that I needed to practice the art of focusing my mind on fewer things that truly mattered to me.

With the book *First Things First* by Stephen Covey in mind, I would sit for five minutes at the beginning of each day to set my intentions, focusing on mindset and habit practice. I would then identify the three most important tasks for the day and complete a two-minute review at the end of the day to reflect on what I had accomplished. Although I initially started with a blank paper journal, I eventually found the motivation to develop a simple tool to help me standardize my practice and make it easier every day. My goal in doing this was to simplify my routine so that I could focus less on building the habit and focus more on benefiting from it. Today, this tool is called the *Daily Focuser*. It is featured at the end of this chapter and also included in the companion guide.

There's a saying that goes, "When everything is important, nothing is important." In my work as a Business Coach, I help leadership teams of entrepreneurial businesses create a clear vision, align the entire organization with where they are going, and create a culture of disciplined execution across the company. It is common for leadership teams to feel overwhelmed by the endless possibilities of what they want to accomplish and then quickly become stressed by trying to do too many things at once. To help these leaders prioritize their efforts, I would coach them to begin with a desired outcome in mind and focus on actioning the first thing—first. I also encourage leaders to keep it simple and focus on fewer initiatives to achieve higher-quality results. In theory, this seems so obvious. However, it can take some time to build discipline around the practice of focus and prioritization.

It was time for me to "walk the talk" on a personal front. There were so many basic life items that I needed to tackle; the enormity of the list was overwhelming. I needed to deal with lawyers, learn how to do taxes, build a team to support my business, and start to form a support network for myself. As I started to simplify my focus on the top three actions each day, I slowly began to get more things accomplished and some much-needed wins on the board.

As I started to catch these wins by using a daily focus ritual to improve my disciplined execution, I observed that several people in my network struggled with their focus and productivity levels as well. Some of my inner circle remarked with amazement that my mood was positive, my days were productive, and I appeared to be making great progress on the path to rebuilding my life despite my circumstances being far from optimal. They asked me what I was doing to help gain forward momentum. My response to them was that I was simply focusing on the most important things and managing my energy effectively.

In my desire to help them realize some of the benefits I was experiencing from my higher levels of disciplined execution, I started to share some of my methods. When sharing my personal energy management practice and daily rituals with them, I would start out by reassuring them that I did not have it all figured out and I was certainly not perfect. However, the practices I had been using were paying off for me and I encouraged them to give them a try. To start with, I shared my *5 Rules* for mindset to help them manage and control their mind. Then, I shared the *5 Habits* to help them choose their behaviors and establish healthy rituals. Lastly, I shared with them the one simple tool that I had been using each day, the *Daily Focuser,* to help them get into the practice of simplifying priorities to gain more momentum and prioritize their needs each day.

Before long, I had established a small community of like-minded individuals who were all enjoying practicing these techniques. They also shared their experiences with each other, and most importantly, they held each other accountable each day. It was magical to see the tools working and the members of the community helping each other along on their journey. With very little effort, it seemed that I was making a huge difference in these beautiful lives. This was the first inkling of a new thought pattern that later emerged into a belief that in helping myself first, I could then help others. As the saying goes about the oxygen mask, I learned that in order to help save others, I needed to first save myself.

Collaborating with others in this way proved to be a great test of my willpower strength to not default into my old pattern of chasing recognition from others or putting the needs of others over my own. With curiosity and compassion for myself, I noticed that something was different this time. This exchange of helping others was not a one-way street. Instead, it was rewarding and uplifting on both sides of the equation. This community soon became a deeply affirming resource and provided me with the motivation to continue to explore additional tools that could be used to help myself and others navigate transition and rise through challenges in their lives.

If you are interested in trying out the Daily Focuser tool, the template has been provided on the following pages, and a downloadable version is included in the free companion guide linked to the QR code included in this book. Further guidance on how to get the most out of the tool is also provided in the free mini-course included with this purchase.

Daily Focuser

When practiced often, this tool has the potential to help you improve your ability to begin each day with your end outcomes in mind. It will help you put more effort into the actions that matter most to you, and it will help you build positive forward momentum in your life. In just five minutes each morning and two minutes each evening, you will soon master the ability to focus and prioritize yourself above all else. My hope is that you, too, will be able to improve your level of disciplined execution each day and experience deeper satisfaction from all you have accomplished each day when you lay your head on the pillow at night.

Caution! As you will have experienced in the past, activating a new habit or personal practice is always challenging at first, and the results are not instantaneous. However, my personal experience and that of others who use the tool has been that the benefits are cumulative and pay off over time. Many have reported feeling that they have a greater sense of control in their day-today life; they feel that they get more of the important things done and are less distracted. Additionally, some have shared that they have achieved greater levels of self-discipline, which has then translated over to other areas of their life. As Martha Beck, American author, life coach, speaker, and sociologist, says, "How you do one thing is how you do everything."

At its core, the *Daily Focuser* is designed to be simple and practical. Frankly, it is less about what you write in the tool and instead more about the space the practice creates for inward dialogue each morning. Rather than rushing to pick up the cell phone or tend to your children, this tool can help you take a few minutes to put yourself first before launching into the day. By simply taking a few minutes to set yourself up for success at the beginning of the day, you will likely experience a deeper presence in your life, greater satisfaction each day, and, of course, more productivity.

Coaching Guidance:

This is now your tool to use at your own discretion and on your own timeline. One thing you may like to consider is leveraging the power of an accountability relationship. If you're interested in establishing an accountability relationship, I suggest sharing a copy of this book and the online resources with them to ensure you're speaking the same language. Then, begin implementing the mindset principles, healthy habits, and the *Daily Focuser* right away. Each one reinforces the others nicely and supports ongoing habit development. Some of the people you may consider playing with in this accountability relationship include a good friend, a supportive spouse, or a like-minded colleague.

Here are some tips to help you get started; however, I encourage you to make it your own and adapt the tool as you please once you have your habit established. One of my mentors, Jonathan Smith, author, speaker, and coach, shared a saying with me early on in my business coaching career journey. He said, "Renee, first learn the rules, then bend the rules, then break the rules."

This is just something to consider as you go about adopting this tool into your day-to-day world.

1. **Begin with a Morning Intention**: A positive, affirming statement about yourself. It may start with "I am a…" or "I believe in…" This technique helps you to practice positive self-talk and appreciation. Examples include: "I am enough," "I am strong," "I am a great mom," "I can do hard things," etc. Several books and podcasts are available that discuss forming positive affirmation statements. If you take a quick peek online, you will be amazed by the enormity of guidance on this. Remember, keep it simple. If you get stuck here, move to the next section.

2. **Set a Mindset Rule Intention:** Next, identify one mindset rule to practice today and define why it is important. The mindset rules that I practice, as referenced in a prior chapter, include: **Be Kind, Be Curious, Be Humble, Be Honest, and Be Grateful**. These rules can empower you to invoke positive thought patterns and inner narratives throughout the day. The book that inspired me here was *The Four Agreements* by Miguel Ruiz. You may consider checking it out.

3. **Choose a Habit Intention:** Identify one healthy habit to practice today and define why it's helpful. As mentioned in the previous chapter, there are *5 Habits* that I use to help me elevate my energy and build capacity; they are: **Daily Stillness, Solution Focus, Plan Ahead, See Progress, and Playtime**. You won't have to look far to find resources that validate the importance of positive habit-building. The material that impacted me the most was *Atomic Habits* by James Clear.

4. **Commit to Three Key Actions:** Identify one to three high-priority actions or tasks to prioritize above all else today. This helps to ensure that your personal needs are prioritized above all else and reinforces

the principle that when everything matters, nothing matters. It is important that the key actions are highly achievable and realistic to accomplish in the day. Many of us tend to fill our daily plate with too many things, then we get overwhelmed and complete very little in the end. The book *Essentialism* by Greg Mckeown helped me understand the power of focusing on fewer things in order to get more done.

5. **Make Time for Evening Reflection:** Lastly, before you head to bed at night, take a moment to sit and reflect on your day. It can be helpful to recognize your accomplishments, identify how you grew today, and identify ways that you made a positive impact on the world around you. The ability to see progress can also help you to form an optimism bias toward positive action and give you the fuel to carry the practice forward and start the new day ahead with focus.

DAILY FOCUSER

MORNING AFFIRMATION

RULE INTENTION

KEY ACTIONS TODAY

1

2

3

HABIT INTENTION

EVENING REFLECTION

CHAPTER 6

PLANNING TO SUCCEED

Over time, my mini-personal practice of simple mindset rules, practical habits, and the *Daily Focuser* tool started to have a positive impact on me and the quality of my life. I experienced greater mental focus, my energy levels elevated, and I started to gain some positive forward momentum on my path forward on my journey to rebuild my life. What had seemed near impossible to accomplish on a daily basis just a few months prior was now my new normal.

As I slowly moved beyond those early stages of survival following the devastating loss of my family and security, my personal practice started to give me a sense of stability and control over my life moving forward. So much so that I started to believe that, in time, I could not just survive, but also thrive and possibly even rise up to access a much bigger life than anything I had previously imagined.

The more I practiced my energy management methods, the more my appetite grew for larger goals and deeper enrichment in my life. In the past, I had not allowed myself to dream big for two reasons: first, I had my eyes squarely focused on the needs of others around me, and second, I did not feel that I was worthy of extraordinariness. Previously, I had convinced myself that in life, "you get what you get, and you don't get upset." However, the positive results I started to gain from managing my energy gave me the awareness that I had more control and influence over my path forward than I first thought. It even seemed possible that once I figured out what I wanted in my life, I could very well achieve it all—and more—if I focused on what I truly wanted and allowed myself to succeed.

In the media, I had read about many personal turnaround stories in which a particular person had hit rock bottom, experienced an awakening, and then went on to significantly transform themselves and their circumstances. I was hungry for more and wondered if I could do that too. At the very least, I knew I was both ready and capable of more, so I decided to take on bigger goals and pursue larger aspirations, and at the very least, give myself the chance to succeed.

As I sat in quiet contemplation about what might be possible for me in the future, I started to write down a list of the things I desired and the goals I wanted to accomplish in my life. Once I started writing, my dreams and aspirations that I had held pent up for decades, came flooding out of me. All of my pent-up desires that I had held captive inside of myself for decades came rushing out. As I reviewed the list, I realized that there was no limit to what was possible for me. Some of the things I wrote down included having my children return home to my heart, rebuilding my financial security, creating a scalable business with a team to support it, becoming a business thought leader, and publishing a book.

In the thick of the dumpster fire of my life, there was no way I could have imagined a future for myself at all, let alone an independent and abundant life filled with health, happiness, and positive impact.

In the past, I had doubted my ability to achieve anything more than what others expected of me, and during the years of my marriage, I had convinced myself that I was not capable of achieving anything on my own without the guidance of my husband. For the 15 years of our marriage, I had conditioned myself to believe that my husband was the center of the universe and that he was far more intelligent and capable than I was. Rather than stand out on my own two feet, I stepped in line and put my energy into serving him as his housekeeper, his caretaker, and his homemaker. Having spent so many years in the passenger seat of my marriage, it felt uncomfortable and overwhelming to find myself in the driving seat and take the wheel of my life. Although it was what I had wanted, I felt trepidation about my ability to do it all alone.

This hunger for life had me so highly motivated that I wanted to tackle it all at once. My sense of urgency was high, and I wanted to make it all happen immediately. At times I became impatient and frustrated that things were not coming fast enough. Fortunately, my awareness about putting the first things first and taking it one step at a time would set back in and ease my frustration. There was a real risk that I might try to take on too much, too quickly, and crash like I had so many times in the past. Despite my internal drive to move quickly, I could see that I was at risk of slipping into my past patterns of overachievement and burnout if I did not slow down and take it one step at a time.

As shared earlier in this book, in the past, I had a pattern of setting unreasonable expectations and unrealistic goals for myself. Although my hunger for achievement was coming from a place of seeking the approval and acceptance of others on the path to achievement, I would often become so obsessed about the goal that I would disconnect myself from others and go to every length possible to achieve the desired result. No matter how hard I pushed, I never felt as though it was enough, and then, even after achieving success, I would keep pushing until I reached my breaking point. Consequently, each of my peaks of success was met with burnout and deep loneliness when I would find myself alone and feeling void. Rather than sitting with my failure and working through it, I would instead shove down my pain, get back up, and move on to the next mission to please.

Time and time again, academically, professionally, and athletically, I would pursue enormous targets, push myself beyond my limits, and then burn out and find myself feeling bruised, lost, and empty inside. After losing my entire world during my devastating divorce process, I then looked around and discovered that there was no one left to prove myself to, no one left to please, and no one was dictating the terms.

This time would need to be different. I could not afford another fall or episode of burnout. I could not afford to make the same mistakes in chasing the acceptance of others. This path forward to greatness would have to be for my own sake this time and by my own design.

As I started to explore my own desires and goals for a big, abundant, and impactful life, there were times that I felt selfish. Sometimes, I worried about how others may perceive me for moving forward with my life when I had created such a mess behind me. I also worried that my children might think I was moving on to my big life without them. It was true that I risked my children thinking that way, especially since I wasn't there to control the narrative they were hearing at their dad's house. On the flip side, I worried they might grow up never truly knowing who I was and, even worse, without an example of the extraordinary life I envisioned for them. I wanted them each to grow up to become confident, independent, and successful adults who were free to pursue their dreams. If I did not set that example for them, then they may not believe it was possible for them.

Despite the risk to my reputation, I felt it was the right thing to do to lead the way for my children and live my desired life by my own design. In my heart, I knew it was the right thing for me to charge forward to become the best possible version of myself and to live my happy and fulfilled life. Rather than defaulting to what I thought I should do, my commitment to myself this time was to pursue goals that were in alignment with what I truly desired for my own sake. Although I had positive intentions and plans to move forward on my journey, I believed that by honoring myself, I would be able to become a better mom, colleague, and, one day, lover. Sadly, there were many people from my past who did not agree. It was heartbreaking to hear that my children were being told lies and toxic stories about me. There was nothing I could do to protect them from the labels and names I was being called that included such things as a liar, a cheat, a fake, and much more.

Sadly, my ex-husband and his inner circle of family and friends could not hold back their judgments and criticism of me in the presence of my children. Their grandmother cut me out of photos on the wall and in the photo albums in an effort to erase me completely and act as though I never even existed. One of their aunts even went so far as to suggest that they print t-shirts with a photo of me on them and graffiti slanderous words all over my face, as though they were going to form some sort of hate club in my honor.

Although I was not at the dinner table to hear the words myself, the echoes of the past years of listening to my husband's family shame and slander others still bounced around in my mind. The verbal attacks were not limited to people outside the family. Often, members of the family would personally attack each other face-to-face. Sadly, I also received my own share of hate-filled attacks from my husband. In the last five years of our marriage, he would regularly raise his voice and accuse me of being selfish, an inadequate wife, and a bad mom because, in his mind, I put my work over the family. He did not like the fact that my work took time away from him and the children, and he did not hold back telling me all about how he felt.

When I would think about the past and present things being said about me, there were times that my confidence would wane, and I would start to wonder if they were right. Maybe I was selfish after all; perhaps I was a fraud, and it was possible that I was delusional in pursuing my big life. Then I would catch myself and remember wise words shared with me by one of my favorite coaches who said, "Renee, the opinions of others are none of your business." After some self-reasoning, I would then choose to lean into my mindset rules and regain control of my mind, which would then help me rise above the slander and attacks. I came to accept that I could not control what others did or said. Although it hurt deeply, I chose to focus on what I could control: my goals and my path forward.

In my work, I also saw many of my entrepreneurial clients struggle with self-worthiness and their fear of success. Often, my clients would surround themselves with obstacles to success and shy away from taking risks. Although they would try to say that they were afraid of failure, I would point out that, in many cases, they were setting themselves up to fail. Then, as we would slowly unpack that conversation a little more, I would find myself asking the real question that they had been avoiding: "Why are you afraid to succeed?" Some feared that they would be judged by their family and friends for being materialistic or self-serving, others worried that they might make enemies who may try to hurt them on their path, and then some were simply afraid of the unknown because they had never achieved high levels of success.

Out of fear of the perceived consequences or risks of success, most would then often default to their baseline of happiness and hold themselves back from their greatness. It is true that the path to greatness requires us to make tough decisions and often do things that people with a limited mindset may not support. The risks of being criticized for being selfish, rejected for being different, or abandoned at the top are high. However, the rewards can be even greater if we dare to take up the challenge. The question then becomes whether the rewards are worth taking the risk. When I ask entrepreneurs if they are more afraid of the status quo than of change, most realize that the real risk to themselves and their future fulfillment is inaction.

Change is then the only path forward. As I looked up ahead on my mountain climb, I had a tough conversation to have with myself: *Was I ready to take the risk, make the changes, and allow myself to succeed? Would I dare to step forward toward my beautiful life and risk the consequences?* With no fallback plan and nothing left to lose, I decided that it was my time for greatness; it was my time to rise.

With my commitment to myself in mind, I got to work establishing my long-range goals and putting pen to paper to solidify my plans to get there. Some of the goals that I set seemed overwhelming at first, but then it occurred to me that I could borrow from my business coaching toolkit to create smaller milestones targets and a 90-day world of goal setting and execution to help me get there one step at a time. Previously in my work, I had seen leaders set big annual goals and then use the 90-day world of planning and goal setting to help them gain traction toward their goals. In business, this 90-day world of execution had been proven many times over. It made sense that this would likely work for me. At the very least, it was worth a try.

This shift was a huge step up for me; moving from my daily intentions to 90-day goals was a leap, but I felt I was ready for it, and I simply could not make progress toward my bigger aspirations if I did not start somewhere.

> *"If you fail to plan, you are planning to fail."*
> – Benjamin Franklin

There were many things I needed to do to move forward on my journey, and I knew that inaction was my risk. So I got to work putting this 90-day planning setting process to the test by tackling some of my imminent needs first, such as finding a secure roof over my head—a place to call home. With that in mind, one of my first 90-day goals was to relocate from Whistler back to the city of Vancouver and find a space to call home. Although it felt scary to leave the comfort of the mountains in Whistler, my children had moved to the city of Vancouver, and I needed to go down with them to ensure that I would be close by in case they needed or wanted me.

Making the move from Whistler to resume a life back in the city was no small task. Although this goal may not seem like a big deal for many, it was an enormous undertaking for me. Aside from the emotional implications of leaving behind my community in Whistler and uprooting myself once again, on the practical side of things, I was starting from ground zero, and I had no idea where to start. In the past, my husband and his family had controlled the decisions about where we would live, what renovations would be done, what furniture we would have, and so on. This was all new to me. Although I was out of my comfort zone, I had committed to the goal with a clear end in mind and went about executing it.

The first step was to research how to go about leasing a condo. I had no idea what websites to use, what paperwork I needed, and what to expect throughout the process. This was a completely different experience from living in Whistler, where everything was done informally and via word of mouth. I was a nobody in the city and would need to figure out the system quickly because time was ticking. I got to work taking it one milestone at a time and eventually stumbled my way through the process. Before long, I had secured a space to rent, completed an Ikea furniture order, and secured a move-in date.

Thankfully, by the time I got the keys and the furniture arrived, my mom was able to get government clearance to leave Australia during the pandemic lockdown and fly out to Vancouver to help me with the move-in process. From the moment she arrived, we went to work unpacking and constructing one Ikea furniture item at a time. We put together bed frames, a dining table and chairs, a couch, and much more, all the way down to kitchen supplies. By the end of multiple days of work, we shed a lot of tears, acquired several blisters, and learned how to read the most complex Ikea instructions. The experience taught me so much; I discovered that although working toward big goals requires a lot of hard work, if I break it down into bite-sized milestones, I can do almost anything I put my mind to. I also learned that asking for help is okay and can lead to better results in less time. The dots were starting to connect for me. I could see that in addition to my daily energy management practices, a personal planning practice every 90 days would help me to work on my life and make progress toward the life I desired.

With a successful move to the city under my belt, I then set my eyes on my next round of goal-setting. As I started to think about what was next, some self-doubt started to creep in. I wondered how long I would be able to keep this up before I would run out of gas or get distracted. I needed a strategy to keep this process moving forward—my big future depended on it. Once again, I leaned on what I had learned in business while helping leadership teams work on their goals. I reminded myself of the advice I had given those teams many times: keep it simple, focus on fewer priorities, establish a planning routine, and allow myself to track my progress.

That's when it hit me: I needed a repeatable process for my personal planning and a timeframe that could help me maintain focus and achieve outcomes consistently. In the business setting I had been teaching the 90-day world of planning and execution for several years. Time and time again, I would coach leaders to set 90-day goals, we would call Rocks, and then motivate them to complete them within the timeframe. It seemed reasonable that this discipline and timeframe could possibly work for me too—surely it could work for me too.

The concept of "Rocks" combines time management principles, goal setting, and prioritization into one simple theory. If you research the analogy, you'll see many common references to a glass jar, rocks, pebbles, sand, and water. The glass jar represents our time in a given week; the rocks symbolize the importance of working on big goals, the pebbles represent day-to-day tasks, the sand signifies the distractions that consume our time, and the water represents all the unaccounted-for stuff that creeps in without our awareness.

Through the Rocks analogy, I built the discipline to keep my Rocks front of mind, and ensuring that I prioritized time to work on them each week was going to be important. If I didn't do these things, I would risk pushing them aside in the busyness of day-to-day life. I created a one-page tool called the *90-Day Driver*. This tool allowed me to identify and commit to my highest priority Rocks and personal commitments every 90 days to keep them front of mind each week. Within the tool, I captured my top three Rocks that I felt would move me forward in my life. When naming each of them, I define the outcome in a specific, measurable, achievable, realistic, and timebound way. I also used the tool to form a small number of specific intentions for the 90-day period to work on my personal growth, health, and relationships with people in my life. This *90-Day Driver* tool quickly became a powerful resource for me to focus my efforts and measure my progress every 90 days. Even with the help of the tool, it did take me some time to master the ability to work "on" my life while also keeping up with living "in" it. Failure and learning came hard and fast. At first, I struggled to complete any of the Rocks. But over time, with practice, I began to get some of them over the line. Even though I was an experienced business coach, it did not mean that I was a perfect specimen of goal execution. I, too, had to build competency and capacity over time.

One of the key lessons I learned quickly was to focus on fewer Rocks and not take on too much. Although I wanted to take on all the Rocks I identified at once, time and time again, I would fail to get my Rocks completed, and I would cause myself frustration. Just as I would coach my entrepreneurs and their teams, less is definitely more. I would need to learn to follow my own advice by keeping it simple and focusing on the most important things first. With that in mind, I decided to start small and focus on just three Rocks instead of ten. From then on, I maintained a 90-day personal planning cycle to help me progress toward the changes I wanted to see in my life. Some of my Rocks included establishing a financial plan and personal budget, some included establishing a wellness routine of workouts and supplements, and others included Rocks to develop professional skills and more.

In its simplest form, this 90-day personal planning practice helped me to prioritize my goals over other people's needs and gave me the ability to take action each week on the things that move me forward toward my goals. It was not all smooth sailing at first; there were many times that I did not complete all of my Rocks. However, over time, with consistency, this practice got a lot easier and helped me to make leaps and bounds of progress toward my goals.

Coaching Guidance:

If you have the desire to take action and start planning to succeed in your life toward big goals, you may want to consider starting with a 90-day personal planning cadence and setting your first one to three Rocks. If you are coming up blank as to where to focus and what to prioritize, you may want to take a close look at the things in your life that are not working for you and that you do have control over. Perhaps there is a habit you want to kick or a commitment you want to wind down. By tackling your challenges first, you will create more capacity to then focus on the upgrades you want to make in your life.

In the free companion guide linked to the QR code, you will find a copy of the 90-Day Driver Tool and guidance on how you may like to go about using it. Additionally, the mini-course includes a short video to assist with your implementation process. To help get you get started with setting Rocks, I have provided a short, concise, 5-step process for you to reference. My hope is that these steps will help you to gain traction and build confidence quickly.

1. **Assess:** What is working and not working out well for you in your life? Consider both the personal and professional realms of your life. Shortlist actionable changes you would like to make. Be specific.
2. **Identify:** Choose the top three priorities that will help you move toward your aspirations for positive change in your life.
3. **Commit:** Define each of the Rocks as S.M.A.R.T., which means be *specific* about what it looks like when it's done, make it *measurable* so you can conclude that it's done, ensure that it's *attainable* based on your resources, make sure it's *realistic*, and tie it to a *timeframe* to give yourself a deadline.
4. **Progress**: Throughout the 90-day period of execution, check in on your progress each week and make commitments to work on your Rocks each week. Remember, they must be prioritized first.
5. **Assess:** At the due date, assess what has been completed. Even if you do not get all of the way done, it is important to recognize your progress and accomplishments. Capture a list of the remaining work tied to the incomplete Rocks and consider these items as a starting place shortlist for your next round of Rocks.

90-DAY DRIVER

YEAR 2 0 ☐ ☐
QUARTER ☐1 ☐2 ☐3 ☐4

Future Date:

TARGET ONE — SMART Y/N

TARGET TWO — SMART Y/N

TARGET THREE — SMART Y/N

CONNECT TO THE CORE :

ROCK 1

ROCK 2

ROCK 3

GROWTH FOCUS

HEALTH FOCUS

PEOPLE FOCUS

CHAPTER 7

MAKING PROGRESS

In the early stages of building my personal energy management practice, there were times that I fell out of my rhythm, and occasionally, some of my Rocks would also fall off track. These setbacks would sometimes cause me to question my capabilities and cause me to feel disenchanted. Though, on some level, I knew I was making progress, my inability to see it became problematic for my confidence level. I had no clear way to measure my progress and lacked a yardstick against which to measure myself. The only feedback I received was my mom regularly saying, "You are doing so well, darling!" But I often wondered, *Was I really?*

While living alone, I lacked feedback and reassurance from another person. Without input from anyone else, I would occasionally fall into the trap of comparing myself to others and get caught up in an "I'm not good enough" head spin. Then, one day, while listening to a fellow coach beat themselves up over their lack of success in building their business and comparing themselves to others who were crushing their numbers, I found myself advising them not to compare themselves against others because they would miss out on receiving the inner satisfaction from the progress they were making. This was advice that I also needed to heed. In truth, I had not known anyone who had been through a similar situation that I was navigating through. There really was no one to compare myself to, and clearly, there was no value in that exercise anyway. In reality, I was doing the work, putting in the reps, and making progress each and every day; I needed to give myself some credit.

> *"Comparison is the thief of joy."*
> – President Theodore Roosevelt

With the help of my energy management techniques and my 90-day planning, I was able to continue to grow my company, be a great mom, take care of my health, and steadily work on improving the quality of my life. As I thought back to my Whistler athlete friends, I reminded myself that the goal was to focus on continuously improving myself each day; the results would come as a byproduct of the work I did on myself each day.

As a young athlete myself, netball was my game back then, and I had the privilege of being trained by some of the country's top coaches. Over my thirteen years as a netball player, there was one coach in particular who had a lasting impact on me. Her name was Evelyn. She was stoic, firm, and consistent. Her coaching philosophy was clear: *Better today than yesterday.* Evelyn reiterated that the primary goal was not to win games, but to become great athletes. This meant showing up for practice, working on our basic skills, being early for games, and always doing our best. At the time, this felt painstakingly boring, but she was right. Week after week, season after season, together, we got better as athletes and as a team. Yes, we won games (a lot of them… my parents still have the trophy cabinet to prove it), but the key lesson Evelyn taught me was to focus on the *progress* rather than the *results*.

Even with Evelyn's guidance in mind, I did also worry that I may default to my past pattern of trying too hard and pushing myself beyond my limits. In the past, this had not gone so well for me. I had a long track record of setting the bar too high, overdoing it, and crashing due to burnout. I wondered if I was going to keep my unreasonable expectations at bay this time.

As a child, I was extremely academically motivated because I wanted to make my parents and teachers proud. I achieved an A+ average year over year. As a true overachiever, I believed that anything less than an A+ was a failure. In order to maintain my success, I studied relentlessly, passed over opportunities to party with friends, and pushed myself to great lengths to achieve my goals.

In twelfth grade, the academic stress that I put on myself became too much, and I cracked under the pressure. I pushed myself too hard and had a breakdown in the middle of my final grade exams. In the middle of my final math exam, the same terror and panic from the bullying incident several years earlier took hold of my body. My brain stopped working, my mouth filled with metallic saliva, and I got up and ran out of the exam hall. Everyone was shocked and taken aback by what happened. This triggered a series of therapy sessions and meetings at the school. The consistent message of these meetings was that my standards for myself were too high—I was expecting too much of myself. The shame and guilt consumed me. I wanted all of the meetings to end, so I convinced everyone that I would lower my expectations, go easy on myself, and learn from my mistakes.

Though I convinced my teachers and parents that I was fine and "fixed" back then, the unfortunate reality was that it took many more crashes and breakdowns along my adult life journey before I was ready to break my pattern. Losing my family was the last fall that gave me a reason to change my ways. So as I sat looking at my path ahead, I did so with the awareness that I needed to find a healthier way to set reasonable expectations for myself and give myself the ability to see my progress, even if small.

Fortunately, I was introduced to the work of Dan Sullivan, the founder of Strategic Coach and one of the world's leading entrepreneurial coaches. Dan and Dr. Benjamin Hardy wrote a powerful book called *The Gap and the Gain*. In this book, they unpack the science of measuring progress and what is driving that progress ("Gains") and avoid dwelling on past failures and anticipated shortcomings ("Gaps"). This book and the strategies captured in it gave me a lens through which to understand my thoughts and develop strategies to shift my thinking to regularly see my progress and recognize my gains. It became clear through studying their work that I would need a tool or technique to create a more regular cadence to observe my progress and keep my inner critic at bay to motivate me to keep going. That's when I discovered the power of weekly planning and reflection as a personal practice.

Though I had read about a weekly planning practice many times before, it was not until this last time that it finally clicked for me. However, I told myself I did not have time for it, and perhaps, if I am honest, I was likely avoiding putting myself under the microscope of my inner critic each week out of fear of being attacked by her. Historically, I had been pretty hard on myself; I would loathe myself for the smallest of mistakes or failures. With this new focus on progress over perfection, it seemed like it was time for a new narrative—one that allowed me to recognize my progress each week, and so I committed to giving this weekly planning practice a try.

One evening, while scrolling through my Instagram feed, I came across a powerful source of validation. Unexpectedly, a random video feed popped up featuring the famous actor Denzel Washington. In the video, Denzel stood at the lectern wearing a graduation gown in front of hundreds of graduating students of Dillard University. In the speech, he shared a powerful message with the students. He stated that dreams were a recipe for disappointment in the absence of two things: commitment and consistency. He said that *commitment* would get you started, but it was *consistency* that would keep you going. This quote turned a light on inside of me. Yes, I was committed to doing the work to build a better me and a better life; however, I needed a strategy to help drive discipline and consistency to ensure I kept moving forward toward my commitments to myself and my dreams.

After exploring a range of options and variations of a tool to help me see my progress, I developed my own *Weekly Planner* tool. Interestingly, the tool became a powerful bridge between the *Daily Focuser* and the *90-Day Driver* that helped me to ensure that both my short-term priorities for the week are addressed while also taking into account the need to take consistent weekly steps toward my Rocks in order to stay on track throughout the quarter. Most importantly, though, the tool provided a powerfully consistent means to recognize my progress toward my Rocks and the extent to which I was able to prioritize myself each week.

With this simple one-page tool, I found it a lot easier to carve out 20 minutes each Sunday to set my intentions and plan ahead for the week. With practice, the tool helped me to become more proactive and productive, and most importantly, it helped me to set realistic expectations and measure my progress each week. Whereas in the past, I had felt that the week would happen *to* me, now, with the help of this tool, I felt as though it was happening *for* me.

The *Weekly Planner* template has been provided at the end of this chapter and is available in the free companion guide that comes with the purchase of this book. **For further guidance on how to get the most out of this tool so that you can gain steady momentum toward your Rocks and see your progress each week, you may like to check out the mini-course that accompanies the companion guide accessible via the QR code at the end of the book.**

Weekly Planner

To help you implement the *Weekly Planner*, I encourage you to schedule a regular time slot of 20-30 minutes each week for you to sit in an uninterrupted environment to complete this exercise. As mentioned previously, the first step is about establishing the rhythm. Next you will want to slowly work up to completing the whole tool, but know that it is perfectly okay to start out by completing just 1-2 sections. As mentioned, it is important that you do not skip past the weekly reflection section before moving on to complete the plan for the week ahead.

Coming up, you will find additional coaching tips to help you get the most out of the tool and, as a result, get what you want out of your week. Rather than starting your Monday on the back foot and feeling like the week is happening to you, this tool can help you get back into the driving seat and get where you want to go by the end of the week.

Coaching Guidance:

Each section of the tool alone can act as a helpful means to focus on what is important and set intentions that can help you take back control of your week, your energy, and your progress. Here are some suggestions about how you may like to think about and use each of the sections of the tool.

1. **Gratitude Statement:** This statement will help you identify the good in your life that you may otherwise gloss over and not appreciate as you go about your day-to-day life. When we allow ourselves to allow the good in our lives into our hearts, we can access deeper joy and satisfaction in life. When we focus on the good in our lives over the things that are not so great, we can choose to have a positive mindset and recognize our progress on our journey.

2. **Self-Appreciation Statement:** This statement will help you to acknowledge your growth and achievements on our personal development journey. It requires a lot of effort to work on ourselves each day, and sometimes, we are so focused on improving our flaws that we do not recognize our achievements and growth. It is important that we take a moment each week to see our progress.

3. **"Rock" Focus:** This part of the tool will help you to break down the 90-day Rocks into milestones that can be actioned each week. It can be challenging to find the time to work on the Rocks identified on your *90-Day Driver*. However, when you break each Rock down into actionable weekly deliverables, you can gain momentum and measure your progress on your path to completion.

4. **Personal Intentions:** It can be easy to get caught up in the busyness of the week and forget about your own needs for personal nourishment and fulfillment. By committing to actions that fuel your need for personal growth, holistic health, and people relationships, you will be able to ensure that you fill your energy tank each week and prioritize yourself over all else.
5. **Progress Reflection:** The final part of the tool provides the opportunity for you to reflect on your achievements and recognize your overall progress made each week. In doing this, you will improve your ability to see the rewards of your efforts and elevate your confidence around your capability to continue to make progress on your own journey toward your own mountain summit.

WEEKLY PLANNER

I AM GRATEFUL FOR:

I AM PROUD OF:

ROCK FOCUS	GROWTH FOCUS
	HEALTH FOCUS
	PEOPLE FOCUS
REFLECTIONS FROM THE WEEK	

CHAPTER 8

BECOMING MYSELF

Although my outer world was still complex, messy, and uncertain, the basic tools and disciplines that I had been working with were helping me to find my footing and inner steadiness. My mind was becoming clearer by the week, and my actions were far more intentional than ever before. For the first time in my life, I felt in control of my destiny, living my life for my own sake.

There was still a lot of work ahead of me, but overall, I felt I was making great progress. I had settled into my city life and found a space to call home. I had started to build healthier relationships with each of my three children. My business had grown, and my professional reputation continued to elevate. This was a lot more than I could have imagined just months prior. My tools, rules, and habits were helping me to manage my energy and get the results I wanted in my life.

While I was happy with all of the progress I was making along my climb up the mountain of rebuilding my life, I had a sense that I was only scratching the surface of the real work I was going to need to tackle at some point, my inner work. Once again, while scrolling Instagram, I discovered a quote that spoke to this loud and clear. It said, *"The real work is the work you are avoiding."* This message made me wonder what I might be avoiding and why I was dancing around "the real work." What did that even mean, anyway?

Then, one evening, during a call with a coach that my brother had referred me to, his name was JK, he asked a question that helped me understand that I had a lot of unanswered questions to address about who I was, what I wanted and where I was going with my life.

Within moments of starting the call with JK, who was based out of Sydney, Australia, I went from feeling fairly confident about my progress to realizing that I was just getting started. This shift was triggered by a simple question that JK asked me: "Renee, who are you going to become on the other side of this? When the war is over, and the fire stops burning, who will you become?" Dang! It was immediately apparent that I did not have the answers. Frankly, I had never contemplated who I could become in this life, on my own terms, because I had spent my life up until this point being who I thought others wanted me to be.

That one conversation helped me recognize that I had put all of my attention into my imminent fight for survival and need for stability in my life and relationships; however, I had not yet started to tackle the bigger questions that lay ahead of me. The truth was that I had no idea who I really was, what my purpose in life was all about, and where I wanted to go with my life long term. This made me think of the quote from Yogi Berra, "If you don't know where you are going, you will end up somewhere else." Moreover, it seemed that if I did not know who I was, I may risk continuing to try to be someone else. It was time to tackle the inner work—there was no avoiding it. Looking toward a future of independence and personal freedom was both exciting and terrifying. I was in the driver's seat of my life now; however, if I did not know who I really was. Therefore, how could I possibly know what I truly wanted in my life? Sure, I had some aspirations for the future about the relationship I desired with my children, the business I wanted to build, and the book I wanted to write, but that was not going to be enough. I was going to need to go deeper to unlock the real version of me that had been kept hidden for so long.

Whereas in the past, I may have been completely disarmed by the reality of my situation, fortunately, now my energy management practices were helping me to build the capacity to work on myself and my life. Though I had, until this point, put my focus on rebuilding my life, it only made sense that it was now time to focus on reclaiming my identity.

Once again, I leaned into my business system tools and my extensive library of books and podcasts for guidance. It soon became clear that I had a number of tools in my toolbelt that I could convert from business use to personal application for my own benefit. Furthermore, I had a lot of experience helping entrepreneurs and their teams establish their organizational identity, define their culture, and build their core ideology. Through the process of identifying their company identity and vision, I would then help the leaders align all of the human energy in the organization toward that clear vision and instill tools and disciplines to help them execute the vision as a healthy and united team.

The approach I used to help leaders create organizational clarity with the Entrepreneurial Operating System was simple, practical, and concise. We would start with the core values and then identify the purpose and the superior skill of the company. All of this work would help the leadership team to articulate the core ideology of the business—its identity.

In working with teams to select and operationalize their core values, we would draw from the work of Patrick Lencioni to identify the characteristics of the right people for the team, name those qualities, and then put them to use when hiring and reviewing team members to ensure that everyone was on board with the company culture. For most leaders, this would prove to be one of the most helpful aspects of the work because they would gain confidence in their ability to build teams of the right people for the company.

Next, we would draw on the work of Jim Collins to identify the company's purpose, cause, or passion—the real reason it exists—and then determine its niche, the area where the business excels. This work would then give the organization a core focus; it could help the leadership team stay focused on what mattered most, and also empower them to make better decisions in the interest of the business. The deeper sense of meaning and purpose would help to draw in more of the right people who were intrinsically aligned with the purpose, which then often translated to a higher level of commitment and loyalty to the company. Then, the identification of the niche, or superior skill, would help them get clear on what they were best at and avoid trying to be all things for all customers. With more focus and intent, the leadership teams would then be able to increase the level of discipline and work on being the best at their craft, avoiding the tendency to try to be a "Jack of all trades and a master of none."

One day, while facilitating a core values discovery exercise with a new team, it occurred to me that I could follow a similar approach to begin my own identity discovery journey. In the business context, once leaders define their core values, they can more confidently make hiring and firing decisions to ensure that they employ the right people in their business who they can both enjoy working with and also achieve great results with. In my own context, it seemed that an understanding of my core values could help me to better understand who I really am and make better decisions about who I surround myself with going forward.

It took several attempts for me to complete this core values exercise. At times, I was frustrated by my lack of clarity; however, I stuck with it and distilled my core values down to a set of four simple attributes. These were **compassion, curiosity, courage,** and **collaboration**. I felt that each core value alone was affirming, but when I considered them all together, I could honestly say that they felt like me. The real me.

Understanding my core values was such a helpful and eye-opening experience. I felt more connected to my inner sense of self. The values also helped me gain clarity on who I should be spending my time with, and they helped me to confidently take action in the relationships that were no longer serving me. I could clearly see that a number of my challenges in relationships, present and past, came from a core value disconnect. No one was right or wrong; we were simply not aligned. With these values in mind, I started to untangle myself from some friendships and client relationships that were out of alignment. It felt great to confidently take action on my own behalf.

This work on core values gave me a strong start on my inner re-discovery journey and fueled me to keep on digging to discover my reason for being, my purpose. Although I had achieved many things in my life, I had typically done them for the sake of others, and as a result, I lacked the feeling of fulfillment that I craved. At this time in my life, I craved more meaning, connection, and enrichment; therefore, it made sense to start to do the work to understand my inner driving force, my "why," as Simon Sinek would put it. When considering the best way to go about this for myself, I once again drew from my business tools to help guide me. In addition to Jim Collins' work, I also dove into Sinek's work to help me identify my inner desire to make a contribution and impact in this life. Treating myself as my own client was a fascinating exercise. I would swing between facilitator and client; some days, we got along well, then other days, we struggled with each other.

In working with entrepreneurs and their leaders to identify their purpose, I would take them on a journey of discovery to help them move beyond the money and what they did and instead ask themselves deeper questions about why the business must exit. As ideas would surface and dialogue would flow, each team would eventually come into alignment with a shared sense of purpose for the business. The purpose statement would articulate the impact the business was here to make in the world. From that point on, every decision they made would have the core purpose in mind. The more energy they put into efforts aligned with their purpose, the greater the impact, and the more they diverted to other things, the more they pulled away from their impact. It simply became a matter of prioritization.

One of my business clients, Daniel, took me up on the challenge of revisiting their core purpose after two years of working together. He had a top-performing car dealership in Western Canada. Initially, his team had come up with the purpose "to achieve automotive excellence," but after hours of digging into what truly motivated them, they discovered their true purpose was to "help people move forward on their journey." Instantly, the energy in the room shifted, and the team went on to not only achieve greater results, but also build a more aligned team and make a deeper impact on their community. My takeaway from this experience was that purpose truly matters!

Using similar principles, I dove into the work of discovering my own core purpose. The work of Simon Sinek helped me to take the business principles that I was familiar with and apply them to my personal life. With a lot of repetition and revision, I eventually landed on a clear statement that defined my intrinsic driving force, my perpetual motivation, which is "to help set people free." The beautiful thing about this discovery was that it related to all aspects of my life, both personally and professionally. I felt the call to action to help unlock people and set them free. With friends, I would often find myself being a voice of guidance to help them move past their limiting beliefs and unlock their potential. In business, I would help owners systemize their world and get what they all ultimately wanted: their freedom. Wow. What an eye-opening experience this turned out to be.

The beautiful byproduct of this discovery was that I could finally start to resist the temptation to respond to every call to action and not jump at every call for help. This core purpose helped me to see that I act as a key for people and situations that are ready to be unlocked. In many cases, the door is not even locked; however, I could see that in situations where the person or the team were not *Ready to Rise*, then I simply could not help. With an increased level of confidence, I was able to politely decline these requests and opportunities because I could see that there was a lack of alignment.

Coming into awareness of my core values and core purpose became a true accelerator on my journey. Understanding these essential parts of my identity helped me to feel more aligned with my inner self than ever before. Whereas in the past, I had experienced an inner and outer disconnect between who I really was and who I thought others wanted me to be, this newfound awareness gave me the confidence that I would be able to honor myself and be my whole self going forward. This discovery also helped me to see that a lot of my challenges in the past had come from a lack of understanding of my core identity and, as a result, an inability to advocate for myself.

With deeper clarity about who I really was and why I was here in this life, I slowly gained the courage to say *no* to the things that were out of alignment with my core sense of self, and *yes* to more things that aligned with my deeper understanding of self. The more I practiced this, the more embodied I felt. As an added benefit, I felt more rewards and fulfillment from the activities and decisions I was making. This awareness was helping me manage and elevate my energy to a whole new level.

Taking this journey inward to understand and reconnect with our true selves is no walk in the park. There are certainly no shortcuts, and no one can do the work for you. As you embark on your journey inward to remember who you really are and identify who you will become on the other side of your current life transition, please be kind and patient with yourself, take it one step at a time, and trust yourself to know the truth. The answers are within you. When you are *Ready to Rise*, you can set yourself free.

Coaching Guidance:

In the essence of my values and in the spirit of my purpose, I would like to give you the opportunity to follow along with my core values and core purpose discovery process. ***If you decide that you would like to try a similar approach to mine, you may also like to follow along with the free companion guide and mini-course that is included in your purchase of this book; both are accessible via the QR code at the beginning and end of this book.***

Core Values Discovery Exercise

This work is about understanding the characteristics and attributes that define your internal value set. These reflect the qualities that you value in yourself and others. As you get more clarification about your values, you will notice that you enjoy spending more time with people who align with these values and less with those who don't. You will also notice that people who you align with at the core values level will more likely elevate your energy and make a net positive contribution to your life.

The exercise that I used to discover my core values was similar to the exercise that Jim Collins calls the Mission to Mars exercise. Here's how it went:

- I identified a small list of people who I would choose to go to Mars with to start life over; these were the people I valued most and would like to start life on Mars with by my side.
- For each person, I then listed two to three attributes that I valued most in them. From that list, I distilled a shortlist of three attributes that were most common and refined them to confirm my core values. I then spent some time defining what each one meant to me and outlined the behaviors that represented each value.
- With the list complete, I then reality-tested the values by assessing each of the core people in my life and discovered that the ones who I aligned with most were the people who shared these values, while the people who frustrated me or agitated me did not share all of my core values.

Once you have identified your core values, they can help you be more selective about the people you say *yes* to spending time with. When we collaborate with values-aligned people, you will typically find that there is more ease and flow in the relationship, and spending time with these people is typically uplifting rather than deflating. The greater the level of alignment, the better the outcomes for all.

Core Purpose Discovery:

It is important to understand your internal intrinsic driving force and identify your reason for being. This underlying sense of purpose can help you to move through hard things and stay committed to future outcomes because you will know why it is important to keep going. It can also help motivate you to pursue big goals and give you a deeper sense of connection as to why you are here in this lifetime. Understanding this core purpose can help you be more impactful in your endeavors and unlock a deeper sense of meaning and motivation in all that you do. Understanding your personal core purpose can also help you more confidently say no to initiatives or projects that are not in alignment with your own purpose. The more you think, speak, and act in alignment with your purpose, the more ease you are likely to experience in life. The goal here is to create more satisfaction and fulfillment in your daily life and trust in the fact that your life matters.

The approach I took to discover my purpose was drawn from the work of both Simon Sinek in *Find Your Why* and Jim Collins in *Good to Great*. In simple terms, it went like this:

- I identified five pivotal moments in my life and how they shaped me.
- I then built a list of themes that showed up in the sequence of events and tried to focus on naming the motivating force that helped me to move forward on my journey.
- Based on these themes, I then asked myself what contribution I had the desire to make and what impact I wanted to make in the world based on these themes.
- From there, I began writing out a series of statements that started out with the words, "I am here to…" I repeated this over and over until one statement stuck: "I am here to set people free."
- Lastly, I assessed all of the things I had going on around me and the goals I wanted to accomplish and used this purpose statement to help me assess what really mattered to me. In doing so, it became clear that there were many things that I had been doing that were for someone else's purpose, and this awareness gave me the courage to start to pull back from all of the things that did not align with my core purpose.

Once you have taken the time to develop your core purpose statement, it can be used to help you focus more of your energy toward doing the things that align with your inner motivation and that fuel your soul. This awareness can help you slowly start to unwind the commitments that do not align with your inner driving force and purpose. Doing more of what fuels you will give you more energy and motivation and help you rise up to your higher potential. What is good for you, is good for all.

CHAPTER 9

LIFE BY DESIGN

At last, I could answer the question about who I would become on the other side of my transition: I would become myself. For the first time in my life, I felt I knew who I really was at the core, and I accepted myself for all that I was. At last, I was ready to move forward in life as my genuine self. The bigger question then became: *What did I want my big, beautiful life to look like?*

The contrast between living a codependent married life and living a fully independent and unlimited life of my own could not have been more different. Previously, there had been clear rules and expectations imposed upon me. Then, in contrast, as an independent woman, I could do anything I wanted; there were no rules, and the playing field was wide open. There were times when it all felt surreal; I would often have to pinch myself to confirm that it was not a dream. Whereas I may have doubted my ability to do this on my own, for the first time, I felt that I understood who I really was and believed in my capability to embrace my freedom to live my life by my own design.

Over time, I became more and more comfortable with my freedom and started to gain the courage to think bigger about the kind of life I wanted. There had been a time many years prior when I dreamed of having a big life of influence and impact as a Life Coach. I aspired to be on stage, inspiring people to achieve their dreams and working with them one-on-one, helping them achieve their goals. At the time, I had no examples of people who had done that, and my family and teachers may not have supported my dream, so I parked it and pursued a more traditional and secure career path.

My parents were modest people. They lived in a trailer to save up for their first home deposit; they worked hard and valued the security of working for the government in public service roles. Although they were both paid very little for their contribution, they managed to always have enough to provide everything that my brother and I needed. Slowly, after years of hard work, they were able to build a foundation of transferable wealth that they would one day be able to share with my brother and I, and our children. Although I had aspirations of my own, I chose a safe and reliable professional path as an Accountant because I did not want to disappoint them or let them down after everything they had done for me.

From Grade 9, I had shown an affinity for business and accounting at school. One of my teachers called it early that she thought I should pursue a business degree and seek to work for one of the Big 4 accounting firms—Deloitte, PwC (PricewaterhouseCoopers), EY (Ernst & Young), or KPMG. It seemed like a good idea, and I liked the fact that there were clear rules and a path to results. When I shared my decision to become an accountant, my parents seemed relieved, and that gave me the confirmation that I was on the right path.

Straight out of high school, I began my business degree studies at The University of Melbourne and shortly thereafter applied for a Co-op role at KPMG, one of the top firms in the country. While at the firm, I put my hand up for every opportunity to work on high-profile engagements and take on new challenges. I sought the approval of the managers and partners constantly, and it seemed that the more I met their expectations, the further it took me. However, on the inside, I was struggling. Though I was succeeding, I did not enjoy the work, and I could not see myself doing it long-term. After two years of trying to make it work, I finally mustered up the courage to own my truth and leave the firm.

Shortly after leaving the firm, I met my husband. He was visiting Australia from Canada, and he instantly locked eyes on me when we met at a bar. I loved his big personality, his entrepreneurial drive, his courage, and his confidence in the life he was building back in Canada. He proposed that I get a fresh start and join him in Canada, where he already had a house and had started a business. Without a better plan, I decided to give it a try. I got a work permit visa, purchased an open return ticket, and headed off to embrace the adventure in Vancouver, Canada.

Not long after arriving, I quickly realized that he had a fairly traditional view of relationships and marriage. He was intent on getting married and settling down. He had a clear picture that he would be the breadwinner; he would control our finances; he would choose our social circles, and he would decide where and how we lived. I initially felt relieved by the structured relationship and the clear expectations he had set. However, this limited outlook and rigid set of rules later proved challenging for me as I became hungry for achievement and motivated to have my own voice in the relationship.

In the early years of our relationship, there was no time to talk about values or reconcile our differences in outlook because life threw a lot of challenges at us, so we came together to fight each of the battles. We navigated his cancer journey, multiple rounds of in-vitro fertilization, the strain of building a business, and the demands of his big Italian family. Our plates were full, keeping up with life. Rather than resist it, I chose to toe the line and play the role of his servant wife, a diligent homemaker; once again, I did what I felt was the right thing.

After so many years of following along with my husband's plan, it was not surprising that I struggled at first to fully embrace my independence on the other side of our divorce; I had never allowed myself to choose what I wanted before. Then, as I stood looking out toward the possibilities that lie ahead of me, I wondered if I still had it in me to ignite that dream held so long ago to become a coach and help transform people's lives. Without anyone telling me otherwise, I decided that, at long last, I was ready.

As I allowed myself to lean into all of the possibilities for my big life, I often found myself thinking a lot about my paternal grandmother, Jean, and her tragic story. Though I did not know her in life (she passed away when I was a baby), I always felt as though I knew her in spirit, and the more I learned about her, the more I felt that I could relate to her challenges in life. Although my brother and I were sheltered from conversations about our family's history, I came to understand that Jean had been a free-spirited, global traveler prior to her marriage. Then, when she married a farmer, she found herself confined to an unfamiliar and limited life that she had not imagined for herself. Though she did her part by raising her children and taking care of her hard-working husband, it seemed that her lack of alignment and meaningful connection to her life tipped her over the edge. After a long and painful battle with her mental illness, she eventually succumbed to her condition and tragically ended her life not long after my first birthday.

As the only grandchild she ever had the chance to hold, it seemed she had a special bond with me that carried into her afterlife. As a teenager, I experienced recurring nightmares about my grandmother. Over and over again, I would dream about her being locked in the dining room hutch, screaming and begging me to let her out and set her free. In the dreams, I would see myself asking my family if they could hear her and then realize that they could not—I was the only one. Back then, I didn't understand what the dreams were about—I chalked it up to my overzealous imagination. Then finally, after years of recurring dreams, they finally stopped. I felt insecure about raising the conversation with my dad, so I let it pass and said nothing about it.

Although it seemed like an isolated event at the time, looking back now as an adult, in light of my own personal struggles, it seemed that there might have been something of a spiritual nature taking place in those dreams.

Perhaps Jean was trying to show me her suffering so that I might avoid making similar mistakes. It might have been possible that she wanted to prepare for my own fight for my freedom many years later.

Sadly, Jean did not have the opportunity to change her circumstances and pursue her extraordinary life; she lived in an era where women were kept at home and had a very clear role to play. Back then, she did not have the freedom to break free and pursue the life she truly desired, but I could now. Looking back on my past dreams about my grandmother, it seemed that she may have been coming to me in spirit to warn me of my future entrapment and give me the motivation to fight for my freedom. Fortunately, when that time came at the age of 40, I had the courage to take action and break free. Despite the cost, the loss, the trauma, and the collateral damage caused to my children, I remain convinced that I made the right decision.

From time to time, I would contemplate how things would have played out if I had not broken free from my unhappy marriage. It was a scary thought because, through all of the trauma, conflict, and suppressed emotion, I had become completely void and deeply depressed. I, too, had started to lose my passion for life. Sadly, there were days when my emptiness caused me to question whether I wanted life at all. Without a voice, without dreams, and without a safe space to work through my emotions, I doubted whether I could hold up the brave front and that everything was okay. The very thought of admitting to my husband that I was unhappy felt unbearable, and I wondered if it might be easier to disappear deep into the forest and never return. Every time I felt that way, I would fortunately stop myself from that downward spiral and focus my attention on my beautiful children. They were the jewels of my life, my reason for being, and my strength to help me get through those dark days.

Over the 15 years of our marriage, there were times that I found myself in fight mode, there were long periods of freeze, and then, in the final stages, it was all flight. In the end, my survival instinct kicked in, and I fled—I had to save myself. Taking action from that place of fear and survival left me on the other side of my "double exit"—the marriage and the business—in a position of extreme loss. Without a plan and appropriate support, I lost control of the process, I fatigued quickly, and in the end, I left my chips on the table because I was so desperate for it to be over. He wanted the money; I wanted my freedom. I gave him what he wanted, and I got what I needed.

Despite my losses and painful experiences along the way, I truly believed that my commitment to myself and the work I was doing to pursue my personal freedom would one day become a powerful example for my children and many other people, possibly even my clients. On the other side of my difficult transition, I had found my true self and rekindled my love of life; this was something I wanted for all people, not just myself. However, if I was going to be able to help others choose the life they desired, I would first need to fully embrace my own. After much procrastination, I was finally ready to put pen to paper to create a vision of the big life I desired, by my own design.

As I began brainstorming ideas for my future life, I wondered how far ahead I should plan ahead. Different timeframes came to mind: ten years, three years, and one year all seemed relevant for building my plan. In business, I would teach leaders to consider all three of these timeframes when creating their vision. We would start with the ten-year goal, then work back to a three-year picture, and finally define a small set of S.M.A.R.T. goals for the first year. It made sense for me to follow suit and use all three time frames as well.

Starting with the ten-year outlook, I felt it would be helpful for me to create a vision statement to describe the life I desired a full decade into the future. This was inspired by a call with a client who told me about the work of Bob Biehl, an Executive Mentor who has worked with more than 500 clients himself, and specifically a video of his workshop titled "Decade by Decade." Immediately after the call, I jumped online to look up the workshop on YouTube. Bob's philosophy on life was that throughout each decade of our lives, we move through common stages of growth, maturity, and self-mastery. After watching the video several times, I felt validated that *My Life Design* needed to begin with a ten-year outlook.

After several iterations, I developed a paragraph to describe my future vision of what I wanted my life to look like on my birthday ten years into the future. I described how I intended to be living, what my relationships looked like, what impact I had made in the world, the quality of my life, and my overall well-being. It felt great to be able to see into my future and have something clear to work towards.

This vision of my future gave me the motivation to take action; however, I didn't know where to start. Ten years seemed a long way out; it seemed that I would need something closer within my reach to work toward. My own struggle with knowing where to start in the context of my 10-Year Vision was something I had seen my leadership team clients also have difficulty with. Many questioned whether they would even be working with the company by that time and, therefore, had a hard time connecting present-day actions with the 10-year target. In the business setting, I would then use a 3-Year Picture to help them have something clear and compelling to start working toward. With this in mind, I then went about building my own three-year outlook, which I called "My Painted Picture."

As I went about painting the picture of what I wanted to be true about my life in three years' time, a lot of suppressed desires came pouring out of me. Many of the aspirations and dreams that I had once stopped hoping for could now come out and possibly even come true. I wanted more travel, healthier relationships with my children, a bigger network, greater financial security, a thriving business, a well-respected professional reputation, capacity for philanthropy, time off for vacations, and the foundations of a powerful legacy that would make my children proud.

While creating my three-year outlook, I would occasionally catch myself criticizing my ideas, thinking, *Who do you think you are?* or *That's not possible.* However, I would soon reason with myself and reassure myself that I was worthy of this beautiful life—I had earned it, and I had the strategies to give myself every chance to achieve it. It would not be easy, but I could do it. The more I worked on my vision, the clearer it got, and the more confident I became in my ability to achieve it. It gave me a clear vision for my future, a true sense of direction, and more love for life than I had ever experienced before. I was on the right track to my big life; now, I just needed a plan to get there.

In my work as a business coach, helping business leaders build and execute their grand visions, I would regularly teach leaders to take long-range plans and break them down into annual goals to help them gain traction. In an effort to help leaders understand the importance of putting the first things first, I would reference the metaphor that was common among the triathlete community that says, "How do you eat an elephant? One bite at a time." With this in mind, it seemed obvious that I should take my own advice and distill my 3-Year Plan, *My Painted Picture*, down into a small number of specific, measurable, attainable, realistic, and time-bound (S.M.A.R.T.) annual goals for the year ahead.

With some trial and error, I was able to pull together an annual planning and goal-setting approach that enabled me to set a small number of big goals for the year that I felt would help me make progress toward *My Painted Picture*. I chose to start with just five annual S.M.A.R.T. goals and a small number of quantifiable targets. Though I wanted to take on more, I knew better than to test my limits in the ways I had in the past. Burnout was simply not going to be an option this time around.

With the five annual goals set and clearly defined, I then used my *90-Day Driver,* referenced earlier, to set the appropriate 90-day Rocks that I would need to get started on my goals for the year. Although I had already started using the Rock-setting approach previously, this new level of clarity on my 10-Year Vision, my 3-Year Painted Picture, along with my Big Goals for the year, helped me to gain deeper clarity on what was most important to me and elevated the importance of my Rocks. With my future vision in mind, each Rock became substantially more important to move me forward on my path to live my life by my own design.

The dots were starting to connect in a beautiful way. I felt more clear than ever about who I was and what I wanted my life to look like. I had a plan to get me where I wanted to go, and it felt wonderful to be moving forward with such deep clarity. In an effort to simplify my approach and ensure that I could sustain this progress over time, once again, I got to work to synthesize all of these powerful ingredients into one place, in one tool, which I then called *My Life Design*.

Much like the two-page vision and execution tool I had been using in business for years, the *My Life Design* tool became a two-page personal plan that helped me succinctly capture my core identity, my envisioned future, and my plan to help me get there.

Your copy of the *My Life Design* tool is available for your use in the free companion guide included with your purchase. **You can access the companion guide and additional guidance in the digital mini-course via the QR code featured in this book.**

My Life Design

My hope is that this tool, *My Life Design,* will become an unlocking and uplifting resource for you on your journey to redefine yourself and your life. I hope that this simple format will help you to bring together all of the ingredients you need to get clear on who you are, where you are going, and how you will get there. Although it is a simple tool to understand, it will likely not be easy to complete because it will take some time to unwind your limiting beliefs about who you are and what you are worthy of in this life. I encourage you to take it one section at a time, revise it often, and take the time to get clear because once it comes together, energy will start to align, and amazing changes will start to take place in your life.

The tool covers seven important questions. Each of them alone is powerful and will prove to be revealing; however, when they come together, your vision will become truly compelling. I might even say now, be careful what you commit to because what we focus on expands, and your probability of getting where you want to go in life will increase through the simple act of writing it down.

> *"I think, therefore I am."*
> – René Descartes, 17th-century French philosopher

The *My Life Design* questions include:

1. What are my *Core Values*?
2. What is my *Core Purpose*?
3. What are my *Core Talents*?
4. What is my *10-Year Vision* statement for my life?
5. What is my *Painted Picture* of what I want my life to look like 3 years from now?
6. What are my 5 annual *Big Goals* and key targets for the year ahead?
7. What are my unsolved mysteries and ideas for the future that I could park in my *Think Tank* for future consideration?

Coaching Guidance:

Here are some of my summarized coaching guidance for you to consider as a field guide to help you build out your *My Life Design* with confidence:

- Start early, don't delay. Avoiding this work will simply delay your outcomes.
- Take it one question at a time. Don't rush through it; no one is watching.
- All ideas are worth writing down. Sometimes, you need to work through the bad ideas to get to the good ones; allow all ideas to come forth so you can get to the great ones.

- Move on when you get stuck; you can always come back. There is no need to get frustrated with yourself. If you get stuck, move on and come back to the question after some time to think about it more.
- Let each coat of paint dry before adding more. You may feel the desire to hack away at your ideas and speed up the process; however, it can be helpful to let them sit for a while before applying another coat of paint.
- Bring a buddy along; accountability is powerful. This work can be overwhelming and it is often best done with a friend or professional along for the ride.
- Take action on what you commit to. It is one thing to write down your thoughts; however, change will not happen unless you take action.

Once you have your *My Life Design* up and running, you will find that it acts as a powerful road map; it will help you navigate through decision-making and orient you when you might feel lost or disorientated. Following your *My Life Design* will help to ensure that you stay in alignment with yourself and prioritize what moves you forward to the life you truly desire by your own design.

MY LIFE DESIGN

CORE VALUES
1)
2)
3)

CORE TALENTS
1)
2)
3)

CORE PURPOSE

10 YEAR VISION

3 YEAR PAINTED PICTURE

Future Date:

TARGET ONE	SMART Y/N
TARGET TWO	SMART Y/N
TARGET THREE	SMART Y/N

What does your life look like?

MY LIFE DESIGN

BIG GOALS

Future Date

TARGET ONE

SMART Y/N

TARGET TWO

SMART Y/N

TARGET THREE

SMART Y/N

THINK TANK

Goal 1

Goal 2

Goal 3

Goal 4

Goal 5

CHAPTER 10

A SYSTEM FOR LIVING

Slowly but surely I was starting to make progress on this mountain climb to reclaim my identity and rebuild my life. For the first time, I felt completely present and connected with my inner sense of self and more in love with life than ever before. By paying attention to my thoughts, words, and actions every day, I felt in command of the only thing I truly controlled: my energy, and clear on how to use it for my own advantage. Additionally, through the power of my 90-day world of planning and execution, I was able to make significant progress toward my goals and my vision for my life. It seemed that the more I focused on myself and the more masterful I became in managing my energy, the more I found that the resources I needed to move me forward would then appear in front of me. I was manifesting everything I desired.

Previously, I had read a lot about the power of manifestation. I would hear stories about people who had drastically turned their lives around after a heartbreaking tragedy. The books and podcasts would explain the common principles of manifestation as being rooted in mindfulness, energy management, and intentional personal visioning. As my own reality started to turn around for the better and many of my desired outcomes came into form, I wondered if I had cracked some sort of code for manifestation. There was definitely something powerful taking place.

Some days, I would write down my intentions for the day on my *Daily Focuser* first thing in the morning, and then by lunch, I would receive an unexpected email or a phone call that would reveal the very thing I sought to accomplish that day. One specific morning, I had set an intention to explore a big stage speaking opportunity in the world of exit planning. This aspiration came from a place of wanting to share my purpose of setting people free and my recent lessons and experience from working with some of my clients to build their exit strategy. I had no idea how I was going to pull it off or how many years it would take me to get on stage, but I was committed to finding out. Later that day, I received an unsolicited invitation to speak on a national stage with the Exit Planning Institute, the top-ranking global organization in the field of exit planning advisory. Was it a coincidence or manifestation? Frankly, I didn't care what it was—it was working!

Over time and with practice, the tools, rules, and habits started to weave together and reinforce each other in a beautiful way. The 5 Mindset Rules helped me stay in a positive and motivated headspace every day and open myself up to connection with others. The *5 Habits* helped me to establish basic disciplines and move energy forward toward my goals. The 4 Tools, which later became 5, helped me to organize my day-to-day life and focus my energy on what mattered most to me. Then, the piece that helped it all come together was the 90-day rhythm of planning and execution. I was so pleased with my progress, and the results showed.

Interestingly, I found that each of the tools and disciplines in the framework were helpful on their own; however, when they were all applied consistently and at the same time, the results were significantly greater. As I thought about this more, I recalled the work of Steven Covey in his book *The Seven Habits Of Highly Effective People*. The last time I read the book had been while running a half marathon in Whistler, BC. Listening to books had become a tool I would use to motivate me to run longer distances; so long as my mind was focused on something positive, my body would keep running.

As I came into the last mile of the half marathon, in the shade of the forest and the softness of the forest floor, I reached the final stages of the book in which Steven Covey talked about the power of synergies in the context of habits. He shared that each of the seven habits that he had spoken of in the book was powerful; however, when they were applied together, the results were exponentially greater. It seemed that there was definitely something powerful at play with my energy management practice. Based on my own experience, I could verify that each of the disciplines I had been practicing were working together to create results far greater than any of them alone. I was experiencing the exponential results from the power of synergies, just like the book suggested.

There are far too many examples of this powerful pattern of manifestation in my life to capture here in this book. On a daily basis, I would witness little energy miracles happen so often that they became somewhat normal. Even when challenges would arise, I knew that if I leaned into the disciplines and managed my mind, I could trust that everything would work out as it was intended. I stopped resisting the flow of events in my life and became more comfortable with trusting the process and flow of energy.

Another powerful example of the daily manifestation occurred one weekend after my landlord advised that he wanted to move back into his condo and I would need to find a new place to live. Although the news was unexpected, I knew better than to panic. The next day, I committed to start looking into alternative rental options as one of my actions on my *Daily Focuser*. Later that evening, while enjoying an unplanned sushi dinner out with my daughter, I bumped into an old friend who quickly mentioned that a friend of hers was seeking to rent out her condo in the tower further down the road from where I was living.

The next day, I went to have a walk through the condo, signed the paperwork, and within two weeks, I had moved into the condo with ease and efficiency. Incidentally, the new condo had upgraded amenities, a 24-hour concierge, access to all the stores I could want at the front door, and door-front access to local transit. As it turned out, the move was for the better, and not only did it improve the quality of my life, but it also made spending time with me more attractive for my three teenagers and resulted in them wanting to spend more time with me. It seemed that living above the Nike store had paid off! This experience, among many others, continued to reinforce for me the wonderful power of energy management and manifestation.

The more consistent I stayed in my practice, the better the results. The strides I was making toward rebuilding my life by my own design were noticeable on all fronts. All of my discipline and effort was paying off. My health improved significantly, my children and I reunited at last, my business performed better than ever, and I even found love in a new, wonderful life partner.

Although I was making great progress on my climb up my mountain of personal development, there were days that I fell off track and lost momentum. Sometimes, these setbacks caused me to doubt myself and my ability to sustain this work in the long term. Other times, they motivated me to find a way to ensure they could be maintained long-term. My solution-focused mentality had me convinced that there had to be a way to ensure that this practice could be maintained over time. That's when I clued into the fact that there was a possible solution hiding in plain sight, an approach I had been using for years in business: systems intelligence.

My early introduction to business operating systems came unintentionally. When I first met my husband, he was a young entrepreneur in the throes of starting a new business. He and his friend had grown tired of how their past employer had run the company, and so they decided to go out alone. They launched their own business technology company and were hell-bent on doing a better job than their past boss.

The timing of the launch was not ideal for me as they started the company months prior to my arrival in Canada. For months, I barely saw my then-boyfriend. He pawned me off to the care of his Mother (the matriarch of his Italian family) so that he could focus on the business. While he worked away at the office for long hours, I became his mother's pet project. It felt like I was in some sort of finishing school for young women who needed to learn how to take care of their husbands the "right way." I learned to cook, clean, shop, gossip, attend social outings, and, at all times, ensure that my husband's needs were taken care of.

I understood that the business needed his full attention, and I hoped that, over time, it would all settle down and that we would have time to work on our relationship. Sadly, this hectic business-first way of living became our day-to-day reality. After long days at the office and also driving all over the city doing sales calls, he would come home exhausted, eat, and then spend the evening working on his laptop in front of the television. Most nights, he would fall asleep on the couch with exhaustion. As I lay in bed alone, staring at the ceiling of my new Canadian home, I would come up with ideas to turn our circumstances around. However, they fell on deaf ears when I brought them up with him because he would tell me that I didn't understand. He preferred that stay out of it and let him do his thing.

Sadly, as the years passed, this pattern was maintained and became our normal way of living. The business always came first. What fascinated me most was that although he and his team worked hard and did their best every day, nothing changed, and it did not get any easier. From the outside looking in, they never seemed to find their stride, they struggled to build efficiency, and they lacked structure in the way they ran the business. As a result, the business continued to impose on our lives, and at times, I felt as though the business owned us, not the other way around.

With my bachelor's degree in business and my work experience with several large and well-known corporations, I was convinced that there had to be a better way to run our business. At a point of frustration, I hired myself into the company to get on board and try to help "fix" the business in the hope that it would help fix our imbalanced life. Although I had been warned about working with my husband a few times, I felt compelled to get inside and figure out what was going on. Despite the risks, I took action because I was desperate for change and willing to do whatever it took to make it happen.

Within months of joining the company, I realized that the task at hand was a lot more complicated than I initially thought. It turned out that this was not going to be as simple as implementing a few processes and procedures to drive efficiency; there were deeper organizational issues that needed to be addressed. I quickly realized that I was in over my head, and there was a lot more to it than I first anticipated.

Like most entrepreneurial businesses, our company lacked a clear vision, there was no accountability structure, process documentation was non-existent, there were no communication rhythms in place, and there was an overall general lack of leadership presence. I was overwhelmed by what I saw and did not know where to start. Then, one evening, while talking with my brother, he shared that his company in Australia was using a proven business operating system methodology to help with all of the similar challenges his IT company was experiencing. He suggested that I check out the book *Traction* by Gino Wickman to learn more. At this point, I had no other plan, so I purchased the book.

As I navigated through the pages of the book, tears of relief started pouring out of me. There was hope. It seemed that entrepreneurial businesses hit the ceiling and struggled with the same challenges that we were experiencing. The book helped me understand that many businesses would fail due to these complexities; the fact that we were still standing was close to a miracle. I was adamant that we would not become another statistic; we had sacrificed so much as a family to fail now.

The more I read, the more I understood that the challenges we were experiencing were caused by weaknesses in our business operating system and tied to root issues in a handful of areas in the business. The book explained, simply and practically, the science of a business operating system and how simple tools and disciplines practiced with consistency across the business in a 90-day world of planning and execution could get the business into great shape while also allowing us to gain efficiencies and eventually now have to work so hard to hold the business up and keep it on track. Amen!

The content of the book showed me exactly how to use a handful of tools and disciplines in a simplified systemized approach to strengthen each of the key areas of our business and move to a self-managing business with a clear vision, accountability, and team health. As I went about helping the team implement the foundational tools and disciplines, change started taking place. Over time, we developed a shared vision, a clear accountability structure, and values alignment across the team. We established a data-driven pulse on weekly measurable activities that drive results, enabled quick problem-solving and decisive action, documented and trained all processes, and ensured everyone followed them. Additionally, we created a consistent planning and communication rhythm that kept all circles connected, aligning the entire team to improve the business every 90 days.

Although it was not easy, and there was pushback among the team in the beginning, after a few cycles, the system started to click, and the results showed not only in financial terms but also in the overall health of the company. On a personal level, we were able to reduce the spillover of work into our personal time and take true vacations without being chained to our cell phones.

Having seen the system work in our own business, I thought to myself that all owner-operated businesses needed this system in place, and with that, I discovered my calling to become an EOS Implementer® so that I could help many more business owners get what they wanted from their businesses too. With this practical and proven system, The Entrepreneurial Operating System™, I went on to help many more business owners gain control of their businesses, increase the value of the company, and ultimately get what they wanted from it. Through all of my hours in the session room working with leadership teams, I saw time and time again that with the power of a simple, practical, and proven operating system, leadership teams could unlock more human potential and take their business to the next level.

Having seen the power of systems intelligence change the game for entrepreneurial businesses so many times over, I got to thinking that I might be able to leverage the power of systems intelligence to help me sustain my personal energy management practice and take my life to the next level. It seemed that a systemized approach might also help me to leverage the synergistic power of each of the tools and disciplines I had been practicing, just like Steven Covey had spoken about in his book, so that I could unlock more of my own potential and take my life to a whole new level.

In my search for an existing systemized energy management methodology, I found that there were many different tools and techniques available. However, I was unable to find a simple and holistic framework that could incorporate all of the key ingredients I had been using. So, I went to work to build my own energy management system.

As I got to work methodically weaving together each of the tools, rules, and habits that I had been practicing for months, I had the goal to make it so simple that anyone could start it, and so practical that anyone could keep it going. Throughout the development process, I enjoyed the challenge of connecting the dots between each of the components of the system, ensuring that the habits and rules supported the use of the tools, and on the flip side, ensuring that the tools kept the daily rules and habits front of mind to support daily energy management. As I brought together each of the foundational components into a simple system, I felt like I was building an engine. I had seen my dad do this type of work building engines into the night in the garage. As I sat in my office alone at night in my empty condo, I hoped that one day he would be proud of the "engine," the system I was building.

My goal in building this system was to help make energy management so simple that anyone could do it. Additionally, I wanted to ensure that the system would be able to help people effectively convert a small amount of daily energy investment into game-changing results in their personal transformation journey. Lastly, I wanted to do everything possible to ensure that the system would be self-sustaining to ensure that once people started their implementation journey, they would have a high likelihood of maintaining the work over time.

After many iterations and several rounds of pressure testing, I emerged from my lab, also known as my office, with an extremely simple, practical, and sustainable energy management system that I had proven to work. The two main ingredients that kept the system running were the *5-5-5 Playbook* of *5 Rules, 5 Habits,* and *5 Tools* (note: the 5th tool is coming in the next chapter) and the consistent rhythm of the 90-day planning and execution cycle. It was that simple. The completion of one 90-day period of disciplined execution would then trigger a review and reset for the next 90 days. So long as this rhythm was maintained, the system would sustain itself and build greater efficiency over time.

This systemized energy management practice was paying off for me personally; the more I practiced integrating the tools, rules and habits, the easier it got to maintain the practice. This got me thinking that if I could do it, surely anyone could. Everywhere I looked, people around me were signing up for workshops, doing online programs, attending retreats, hiring coaches, and more. Though they were trying different things, it seemed as though nothing was really working. I found it most difficult to watch people I cared about moving through major life transitions such as turning 40, getting divorced, becoming empty-nesters, changing careers, and selling their businesses.

Though their circumstances were different, the root issues seemed the same for all of them. They were struggling to manage their energy, they had lost sight of who they truly were, and they lacked direction about where they were going next. While they were trying to solve their problems on the surface, I felt that they were stuck because they were not doing the work on the inside. With my new lens on energy management, it seemed that their system was weak, and they lacked the methodology to upgrade it.

"Upgrade your system, upgrade your life."
– Renee Russo

As my peers watched me rise through my adversity and transform myself and my life, they became curious about what I was doing and wanted to learn more. I shared that I was running an energy management system that was helping me to upgrade my energy, upgrade myself, and upgrade my life. The more I shared, the more they wanted in. Without intention, I then found my first clients.

At first, I was hesitant about sharing the system with others; I did not feel it was completely ready for public consumption. But then I realized that through sharing it with others, I would likely gain some meaningful insights and feedback that could help me refine the system so that one day in the future, I could share it more widely. I stepped outside my comfort zone and rose the opportunity to help them gain control of their energy, reclaim their identity, and get what they want in life.

Rather than teach multiple simultaneous implementations, I felt it would be more efficient and effective to run a beta group workshop series to help a small group of my peers integrate the system into their lives. During onboarding workshops, I shared with them each of the tools, rules, and habits of the *5-5-5 Playbook* and helped them establish their daily, weekly, and 90-day rhythm of planning and execution. I enjoyed the experience of teaching and coaching my peers to work with the system; it felt like my vision was coming to life right in front of me.

With every passing month, the beta group members improved their understanding and mastery of the tools, habits, and rules and slowly started to realize the power of energy management in their own lives. They shared that they felt more centered and present in their life; they were able to overcome adversity and rise above the challenges they were facing; they felt confident about where they were heading on their path; and they also started to experience the daily miracles of manifestation show up in their lives.

It was not easy for me to teach this system to others; it was something that I had created, and I felt personally connected to it. It was difficult to hear their constructive feedback and to witness their early struggles to get it.

Despite the discomfort, I carried on and stayed committed to the process of learning how to become the guide they needed to benefit from the system. It could not make it about me; it had to be about them and their journey. Fortunately, over time, they got where they needed to go, and along the way, the system became stronger and more effective in its ability to help transform people's lives. I remain eternally grateful to each and every one of the beautiful humans who helped bring the finishing touches of this system together so that we could share it with the world.

As you contemplate starting your own self-implementation journey of the *Ready to Rise Energy Management System*, I encourage you to keep a few things in mind on your way. First, there are no shortcuts to transforming yourself and your life—it requires a lot of work, along with a high degree of commitment and consistency. Second, energy management is not a single technique; it is a method of integrating simple practices that help you stay focused on what matters most. Lastly, each of the tools, rules, and habits embedded in this system will be helpful on their own, but when they are integrated and applied consistently, you will begin to experience exponential outcomes.

Having seen the power of this simple, practical, and proven system quite literally transform people's lives for the better, I can confidently say that if embraced fully, this energy management system will help you to gain control of your life, upgrade your energy, and realize your freedom to live your life by design. The only thing between where you are and where you want to get to on your climb up your personal mountain is you. Before you start this journey, it is important that you ask yourself whether you are truly *Ready to Rise*.

If your answer is yes, and you feel that you are truly Ready to Rise to your higher potential and take your life to the next level, I encourage you to scan the QR code at the beginning and end of this book to access your free companion guide and digital mini-course to help you get off to a flying start.

CHAPTER 11

EMBRACING FREEDOM

It had not been long ago that I had found myself stripped of my identity and my entire world, sitting at the foothill of the biggest mountain climb of my life. What lay ahead of me was nothing short of terrifying, and the climb up from my dismal state was excruciating. Though I thought about giving up many times over, with the good fortune of my simple and practical tools for energy management, I had enough strength to get up and start moving forward. As I progressed on my journey, drawing upon the power of my simple and practical energy management system, I started to build the confidence that I would not only survive, but also thrive on the other side of my traumatic transition.

Through the practice of consistent energy management techniques, a systemized world of 90-day personal planning, and a compelling vision of the life I desired, everything I needed and wanted, started to come into form. Some may call it magic; I simply call it manifestation. When asked if all the sacrifice and personal loss were worth it, my answer is yes. Why? Because in losing everything I valued at that time in my life, I found the one thing I had been seeking all along—the freedom to be my true self and live the life I truly desired.

In the past, I had hidden behind the needs and expectations of others, afraid to reveal my true self to the world out of fear of rejection and abandonment. But as my personal life fell apart, all the structures I had been hiding within broke down, and my worst fear became my reality. Fortunately, through that experience, I had an awakening moment that encouraged me to finally open the door to the cage I had kept myself captive in and, at last, embrace my freedom to become the person I was born to be and live the extraordinary life I desired.

While navigating my self-re-discovery process, I found peace and validation in the work of Doctor Gabor Maté, author of *The Myth of Normal*. Dr. Maté's words helped me to understand that prior to my "exit," I had been living an exhausting diametric existence for decades. Like so many other people, I spent a lot of my energy trying to conform to the societal "rules" and expectations placed upon me as a young woman and worked hard to tame the "inner child" desire within me to break out and run free. In my efforts to "fit in" to a life of normalcy so that I would be accepted by others, including friends, family, and my husband, I chose to abandon myself, surrender my dreams, and move into personal hiding. For so long, I worked hard to hold up this false front that everything was fine when nothing was fine.

The decision to leave my marriage came from a place of desperation. I could no longer hold up the false production of happiness, and I could no longer conform to this external illusion of normalcy. My fight for freedom became so overwhelming that my survival instinct kicked in and overpowered my mind. I felt that I had one path, and that was to flee. When the breakout day arrived, I was unprepared, under-resourced, and out of control.

The path out of my "caged" life came with devastating loss and extraordinary hardship. There were many times that I felt I could not keep going, but with the help of my personal practice and the desire to one day become the mommy children deserved, I kept on wading through the mess. Then, as I emerged out of the "shit pipe," a reference from the book *The Shawshank Redemption* by Stephen King, shared with me by a good friend, I experienced the most profound level of euphoria—I was finally FREE!

At first, this new world reality of my personal freedom was overwhelming. It felt as though my memory had been erased, as I did not know who I was or what I wanted for my life. Then, as I began my journey inward to learn how to manage my energy, reclaim my identity, and rebuild my life, I fell more deeply in love with myself and grew increasingly hungry for all that was possible on my unlimited journey ahead.

Although igniting, I wondered if this new sense of freedom was going to be something I would be able to sustain over time or if it would wear off after a while. Without truly understanding what freedom meant to me, I feared that I would not be able to uphold it and protect it. I worried that there might be a chance that I may default to my old pattern of living for the sake of others once again. However, I had worked so hard to get to this place that I did not want to risk losing the very thing I had fought for all along—my freedom.

The curiosity to learn more about this concept of freedom and how to maintain it in my life long-term drove me back into my research. Fortunately, I did not have to look far because I quickly discovered the work of Dan Sullivan, author and co-founder of *Strategic Coach* and mentor to Gino Wickman, the founder of *EOS Worldwide*. In his work, Dan talks about four different types of freedom: the freedom of time, money, relationships, and purpose. As a student of his program, I leaned into this philosophy and worked with one of the coaches in the program to help me define what each of the freedoms meant to me. In that process, I learned an important lesson: I would not be able to protect and preserve what I did not understand. Therefore, it would be important for me to continue to do the work to define my own freedoms so that I would then honor and preserve them over time.

With the four freedoms that I had been working on in mind, I became curious about what else freedom could mean to me and how I might be able to weave it into my energy management practice. To help me organize my thoughts, I started a giant word jumble on my six-foot-wide whiteboard in my office. I wrote out every word and definition of freedom that came to mind. I started to group the words into five categories of freedom that resonated with me. These five categories became my five pillars of personal freedom that would soon help me elevate my lived experience of freedom to a whole new level.

These five pillars of freedom that I came up with were the freedom of **people, purpose, growth, wealth, and health**. I then went about deeply defining what each of these freedoms meant and how I wanted to enact them in my life. As I reviewed my own description of each of the pillars of freedom, I discovered that, for the most part, I was already experiencing much of the freedom I desired. In the past, I had told myself that freedom was a destination and dream for the future, but this exercise showed me that freedom could be a lived experience with practice and intention.

My own experience had shown me that the living experience of freedom was a byproduct of managing my energy, embracing my true identity, and empowering myself to go after the life I desired by my own design. Although it sounds simple in theory, I know that embracing freedom is not easy, which is probably why I tackled it last on my journey.

When we spend so much of our lives trying to fit in and follow along with social expectations of how we "should" live life, most of us become disconnected from our true desires and fool ourselves into choosing a "normal" life over freedom. One time, I read a short story about how people would domesticate elephants in the circus. From infancy, the elephants were tied to a short peg in the ground, preventing them from roaming freely. The only time they were released from the peg was under the command and control of their master. Then, as the elephants grew larger and stronger, they continued to be tied to the same peg, unaware that a simple step forward could easily break them free from captivity. Through the process of taming the elephants, they would abandon their hope for a wild and free life, and they would surrender to their life of captivity and never know anything different. Reflecting on this, I realized that my life conditioning had kept me captive in the delusion that a normal and secure life was for the best. I had told myself a lie that a safe career and secure marriage were all that I could expect from my life. Later, on the other side of my break out, I found that the freedom I wanted was not lost; it was there all along. All I needed to do was to take that first step forward by choosing myself.

The decision to leave my marriage stemmed from a deep desire to break free from the internal prison that I had held myself captive in for decades. I had grown tired of trying to be what others wanted and holding up a false front that I was happy. I was not happy, I was not fulfilled, and I was not willing to fake it anymore. In that single act ending the marriage, I did the hardest thing I had ever done in my life—I chose me. I broke the imaginary rope that had held me tied to the peg in the ground for more than a decade. From that point on, freedom was mine for the making. It was not an easy path to access the freedom that I craved, but over time, with discipline, consistency, and a lot of tears, I got there in the end. At last, I was free to be my true self and live the life I desired by my own design.

> *"Freedom starts with choosing self over all else."*
> – Renee Russo

In an effort to help others access their freedom, I felt it was important that I build out the 5th tool in the toolkit, the *Freedom Check-Up*. My objective in creating this tool was to formulate a simple, practical, and repeatable method that could help others define their own five pillars of freedom and then use these definitions to help them focus their daily efforts and energy management practices to realize the freedom they desire.

Interestingly, the very first thing I sought at the beginning of my transformation journey turned out to be the thing that I came to understand last—freedom. Discovering my freedom to love myself and live my life by my design has been the most profound and transformative experience of my life. There were many times along my trek up the mountain that I did not think I would make it; however, as I broke through this final stage of the journey and unlocked my own definition of freedom, I felt that I had, at last, reached the summit.

The summit, it turned out, was not the end of the journey; instead, it was just the beginning of the best chapter of my life, where I continue to embrace my freedom to live my life of freedom every day. While talking with others about my newfound freedom, I would share the tool with them and encourage people to sit and write down what each of the freedoms of purpose, people, growth, health, and wealth meant to them. As an example, I would share my own definition of these freedoms, and eventually, I found myself stringing together one paragraph that brought them together in a concise way. Many would comment that it sounded like something great to work toward. However, I was able to share that with practice I was increasingly living this life more and more every day. One day, while talking with a fellow Exit Planning Advisor, I coined the term my *"Significant Life"* as the name of my five freedoms combined. *My Significant Life* statement goes like this:

> *"In living my Significant Life, I am free to live with deep purpose in everything I do; I am free to cultivate trusting relationships with people who love me as my true self; I am free to perpetually grow and evolve my personal mastery; I am free to establish abundant wealth that I can share with others; and I am free to live with optimal health and holistic well-being for my whole life span."*

Wherever you find yourself on your personal growth journey, no matter what type of transition you find yourself navigating, I encourage you to take the time to consider what you truly desire in your life and what freedom means to you. You cannot realize your freedom—preserve and protect it—if you don't know what it means to you. As you start to define what your own pillars of freedom mean to you, including the freedom of purpose, people, growth, wealth, and health, you will then start to understand what you need to do to get there.

Once you understand what each freedom means to you, and can define your *Significant Life*, it will then become apparent what decisions and actions need to be taken to move you toward your freedoms. The truth is that no one else can give you your freedom; it is yours for the making. Just like that elephant, all you need to do is take that first step forward and choose you.

Freedom Check-Up

I want to give you some brief coaching notes to help you identify what each of the five freedoms means to you and ensure that you are clear on what your own living experience of each one of them looks like for you. ***Also, note that the Freedom Check-Up tool, along with all of the tools and disciplines featured throughout the book, are included in the free companion guide and digital mini-course, which are all accessible via the QR code provided at the beginning and end of this book.*** This tool can help you to identify what each of the five pillars of freedom—*People, Purpose, Growth, Wealth, and Health*—means to you. As you consider each of the five freedoms individually, I encourage you to think about these steps as you move through each pillar:

- Identify what living in this experience of freedom could look like for you in your life; be as specific as you can.
- Describe how you anticipate this lived experience of freedom would allow you to feel; do your best to name your emotions.
- Identify the actions and efforts you could take to help you move toward this lived experience of freedom.

As you start to capture and define what your lived experience of each of these five pillars of freedom could look like for you, consider this: when you act in alignment with your inner desires and your inner truths, you will elevate your energy, boost your enthusiasm, elevate your joy of living, and ultimately allow you to bring more of your best self into the world. You need to trust in the belief that what is good for you is good for those you love and is in the best interests of all who you will encounter in the future.

On a regular basis, at least every 90 days, I recommend taking an extended Daily Stillness break—one of the *5 Habits*—to assess how well you are living into each of the freedoms according to your definition. You may like to use the two-page Freedom Check-Up template on the following pages to help you track your progress.

When using the Freedom Check-Up tool, you may also like to rate your present experience of each freedom on a scale of 1 to 10, with 10 being the highest and 1 the lowest. Once you've completed this for each freedom, you could then form a short list of actionable intentions to help you better align your efforts over the next 90 days with what matters most to you, allowing you to fully embrace your experience of freedom. There's no need to wait; it's yours for the taking right now.

Coaching Guidance:

This exercise of thinking about freedom may be new for you and a little challenging at first. Though uncomfortable, I encourage you to keep working through your inner thought process and keep coming back to the exercise. Below, you will find some coaching suggestions to support your discovery process.

The *Freedom of People* helps you to focus your energy on your inner circle of people who love, support, and uplift you. Spending time with these people helps to increase your positivity and self-image.
- o   Question - What types of people do you enjoy being around, and what do you enjoy doing with them? What are their core values?

The *Freedom of Purpose* helps you to focus your efforts on making contributions to the world, both personally and professionally, that align with your purpose and intrinsic motivating force. As a result, these experiences can help to energize and inspire you.

- o   Question - What are you motivated to contribute to the world? What fuels your soul? How does this manifest in the world around you?

The *Freedom of Growth* helps you to name and prioritize efforts toward the types of learning and development activities that improve your mastery, enhance your talents, and give you the confidence to share your talents with the world.
- o   Question - What forms of learning inspire you? What hobbies do you enjoy? What quenches your thirst for learning?

The *Freedom of Wealth* helps you to value your time and financial resources and spend them wisely and in ways that you feel good about. Having financial and resource security can bring a lot of peace and create the capacity to focus on living rather than earning.
- o   Question - How can you secure your financial future? What do you value spending resources on? What gives you peace of mind about the sufficiency of your resources?

The *Freedom of Health* helps you to name and prioritize activities that elevate your holistic sense of well-being, including the mind, body, and spirit. This awareness can help you remember that it is important to prioritize your health so that you can embrace the richness of life, now and in the future.
- o   Question -What are your physical health needs, and how can you support them? What elevates your mental and spiritual well-being? How can this be maintained?

FREEDOM CHECK-UP

FREEDOM OF PURPOSE

What it looks like for me...

SCORE   /10

FREEDOM OF PEOPLE

What it looks like for me...

SCORE   /10

FREEDOM OF GROWTH

What it looks like for me...

SCORE   /10

FREEDOM OF WEALTH

What it looks like for me...

SCORE   /10

FREEDOM OF HEALTH

What it looks like for me...

SCORE   /10

FREEDOM CHECK-UP

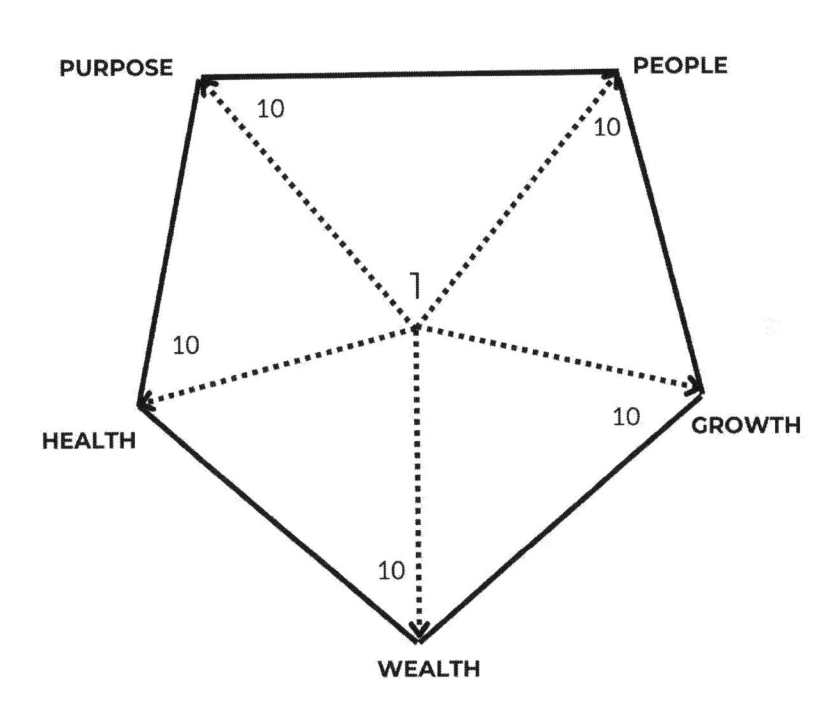

```
           PURPOSE                    PEOPLE
              •10                  10•
                 \               /
                  \             /
                   \           /
                    \    1    /
          10•────────•───────•──10
           /                      \
          /                        \
       HEALTH                    GROWTH
          \                        /
           \                      /
            \       •10          /
             \      |           /
              \     |          /
               \    |         /
                \   ↓        /
                  WEALTH
```

PRIOR TOTAL
DATE: [   ]

CURRENT TOTAL
DATE: [   ]

CHAPTER 12

BECOMING SELFISH

My self-transformation journey has not been easy or smooth. As the saying goes, the path to change is simple in theory, but it's not easy in practice. Even though I'd made the decision to get back up, reclaim myself, and rebuild my life, doing so was a struggle in every way, and the number one challenge I faced was myself. On a daily basis, I battled with negative self-talk, and even with my mindset rules in place, I often felt undeserving of a second chance at life and freedom. The old tapes playing in my mind, combined with the echoes of verbal attacks from my husband and ongoing criticism from his family, made me question my worthiness of the *Significant Life* I craved so deeply.

The ongoing criticism and judgments being spoken of in front of my children were the hardest of all to deal with. Although I initially tried to defend myself and protest these accusations, I soon realized that it was futile. They could not and would not understand. Their small-minded and judgemental behavior was a force beyond my control. It seemed that they did not know me at all and could never comprehend my true intentions in leaving my marriage. They would not understand that in choosing myself, I was saving myself from a life that could not allow me to be free. In breaking the pattern of living my life for the sake of others, I intended to become my true self and be the mother my children deserved—a healthy and happy mom who could love and nurture them fully.

The hard pill for me to swallow about it all was that the people who were saying all of these awful things about me were people who knew better and were well aware of all of the personal sacrifices and contributions I had made in my marriage, my family, and my community. There was no acknowledgment of the fact that, in order to pursue that life with my husband, I had to leave my family back in Australia and everything that I knew in order to give him what he wanted. There was no respect for the fact that during my first year in Canada, I cared for my husband 24 hours a day through his cancer journey and nursed him back to health. There was no appreciation for the fact that I had put myself through multiple rounds of in vitro fertilization and endured birthing traumas, including a late-stage miscarriage, to create our three miracle children. There was no regard for the fact that I had always put the needs of our children, my husband, the family business, and his overwhelming Italian family above my own for 15 years.

For so long, I had felt unseen and unloved. Then, sadly, when I bravely pursued my freedom to become my true self and live my *Significant Life*, I felt completely rejected for it. To many people, my actions appeared selfish. Without knowing the full story, I could understand why people might think that. However, those on the inside who did know the backstory, who knew better, still hung me out to dry. Even though I tried to explain that I was doing this for a good reason—that I could still be a great mom and a successful entrepreneur—my pleas fell on deaf ears.

There were days when I thought about throwing in the towel and giving up on myself. But then I realized that doing so would prove them right, validating the belief that I didn't deserve this extraordinary life. So, despite the attacks, I bravely continued the work to unlock the real me that had been hidden inside for so long and to pursue my *Significant Life*. The only opinions that mattered to me were those of my children. I wanted them to understand where I was coming from and why I was making these changes.

The break in communication with my children made it nearly impossible to share my side of the story with my children. I wanted to explain myself to them but had no way to reach them. Every day, I worried that they were forming negative and irreversible opinions of me. Although I was tempted to hide away in shame and guilt, I chose not to do that because I felt it would be a better use of my energy to focus on becoming the version of me that I wanted them to know in the future, should they ever come home to my arms.

To help me continue my healing journey and to help me work on repairing my relationships with my children, I engaged a multitude of professionals, including therapists, coaches, and counselors. With their help and my unrelenting hope, eventually, communication lines started to open up. With every opportunity to connect, I was able to apologize for my actions, explain my reasons for my decision, and then, as trust started to build, we were able to rebuild our relationships. Over time, they understood that I had not left the family; I had just put the unhealthy marriage to an end, and eventually, they agreed that it was the right thing to do.

Two years into my life transition journey, I was asked to join a fellow coach on a podcast. She wanted to hear my story and create an opportunity for me to share my life lessons with her audience. During the recording of the podcast, Debra dove deep into my personal and professional experiences and asked about my source of motivation. Many words were expressed and tears were shared on both sides. One of the things I remember sharing was that I was compelled to take action because I realized that I did not want life at all if I could not have the life I wanted. I shared that I had reached that place of desperation because I had abandoned my own needs and desires for so long, and it eventually caught up with me. Debra and I both shared difficulty with prioritizing our needs, struggles with our self-confidence, and fear of seeming "selfish" by putting our own needs first.

Instantly, I clicked into coaching mode and unpacked the concept of selfishness live on the podcast. I asked Debra for some examples of actions that made her feel "selfish." She mentioned examples like taking time off, saying no to others, and engaging in self-care activities instead of serving others. I then asked her what she thought the term "-ish" meant, and she replied, "A little bit." I followed up by asking if she believed that doing these actions for herself "a little bit" of the time made her a bad person. Naturally, she responded with, "No." We both laughed at how ridiculous it was to shame ourselves under the illusion that being selfish was a bad thing. Selfish didn't mean self-obsessed; it simply meant allowing yourself to put your own needs first some of the time, recognizing that by doing so, you could become a better version of yourself with more capacity to show up for others and make a difference. We both left the conversation feeling uplifted and encouraged to practice and embrace the art of being selfish a lot more!

With this newfound awareness, and frankly, nothing left to lose, I gave myself permission to be selfish and pursue my *Significant Life*. As a result, my coaching practice began to grow with an influx of new work opportunities and speaking engagements. Additionally, wonderfully kind and generous people started entering my life with a genuine desire to help me succeed. Then, the most amazing thing happened—I fell in love with the man of my dreams. He was the most loving, kind, sensitive, loyal, and brave man I had ever met. It seemed that all of my personal development and energy management work was starting to pay off, and the momentum was further supercharged by my willingness to be selfish and embrace my freedom to live life on my own terms.

One of the kind and generous people who entered my professional life at that time was a successful local businessman named Sid. He and I had met for breakfast a few times, during which he generously mentored me and helped guide some of my decisions on my growth journey. When he invited me to attend a personal planning workshop he was organizing, along with a small cohort of fellow coaches, I eagerly accepted.

On a cold winter Saturday morning, I headed into downtown Vancouver to join more than a hundred attendees for a day of learning, self-inquiry, and personal goal-setting. The learning component of the day focused on exploring strategies to overcome limiting beliefs, which seemed perfectly timed for me, given that I had been working through my own battles with worthiness. Facilitated by Dr. Caitlin Frost of the Rivendell Retreat Centre, BC, we moved through a series of exercises that helped us each understand the root source of our limiting beliefs and then work together to build strategies to overcome the limiting beliefs to ensure that we would not succumb to them.

The exercises helped me see that I was still carrying remnants of the toxic messages from my past that had held me hostage. It became clear that I was still holding on to the limiting belief that my children wouldn't love me if I chose my freedom. The logical side of me knew I had chosen myself in the best interests of all my loved ones and understood that, in order to be the mom I wanted to be, I needed to become the best version of myself. However, the insecure side of me feared that my children would never understand or forgive me for what I had done.

With the support from the room and the guidance of the facilitator, I gained the confidence to reject my limiting beliefs that I had allowed to hold me hostage in the past and embrace my truth that *"I am a good person. When I do the right thing for myself, it is the right thing for others. In time, as my children see, trust, and love the real me, they will one day understand that I did the right thing for all of us—I gave them their real mom."*

As the workshop concluded, my friend Sid came to the front of the room and shared a powerful excerpt from Nelson Mandela's inaugural speech in 1994. It moved me and confirmed that I must continue on this beautiful journey of becoming myself. I hope that it will inspire others to continue to do the work to allow their lights to shine, too.

> *Our deepest fear is not that we are inadequate,*
> *Our deepest fear is that we are powerful beyond measure.*
> *It is our light, not our darkness, that most frightens us.*
> *We ask ourselves, who am I to be brilliant, gorgeous, talented, and fabulous?*

Actually, who are you not to be?
You are a child of God.
Your playing small doesn't serve the world.
There's nothing enlightened about shrinking so that other people won't feel insecure around you.
We were born to make manifest the glory of God that is within us.
It's not just in some of us, it's in everyone.
And as we let our own light shine, we consciously give other people permission
to do the same.
As we are liberated from our own fear, our presence automatically liberates others.

– Marianne Williamson, A Return to Love: Reflections on the Principles of A Course in Miracles

It is my hope that as you come to the end of this chapter, you might feel inspired to challenge your own limiting beliefs about your worthiness of your *Significant Life* and work on reframing your mindset around being selfish. In all of my experience, I can confirm that the only barrier you face is you, and until you recognize that if you don't matter, nothing matters, then you will continue to live your life in captivity, chained to the imaginary peg, as in the elephant story shared earlier. As Marianne Williamson shared, *"Your playing small doesn't serve the world."* It is your time to rise!

CHAPTER 13

HELPING OTHERS RISE

With my purpose in mind—"to help set people free"—I felt a burning desire to share this energy management system with others so that I could help them realize their freedom to live their own *Significant Life*. This yearning to help others was not a new sensation for me. From an early age, I had experienced this insatiable need to help others. At every opportunity, I would put my hand up and volunteer to help anyone and everyone who I encountered. Although it was born in me, it was also something that was nurtured by my parents.

My parents were strong community advocates and volunteers. Both grew up in small country towns and understood the importance of community contribution. They modeled this extensively throughout my childhood, particularly my mom. Whether it was running errands for elderly neighbors, doing people's ironing, helping out at bake sales, or knitting slippers for people, you name it, she was all over it. She didn't just do the small acts of kindness; she also went out of her way to help others in big ways, such as housing a number of my cousins when they came down to the city to attend trade school. One of them came to live with us while he took his carpentry course, and another came to live with us while taking her hairdressing program; guess who became the test dummy for the hairstyles, *yours truly!*

To say I admired my mom's generosity and contribution would be an understatement. I did not just respect her; I wanted to be like her. In her example, I became a *Girl Guide* for many years. I also volunteered at the food stand at the local sports club on Saturdays to help raise money for the football association. Then, as a young adult, I volunteered my time every weekend to visit senior citizens in my neighborhood, helping them avoid feeling lonely. Helping others was simply part of my upbringing.

To this day, my mom continues to go out of her way to help others every day. One time, I called her to do my daily check-in and asked her what she had been up to. She shared that she had just returned from downtown Melbourne, close to where she and my dad live, after having dropped a gentleman off at a men's shelter. I asked her to tell me more about that. She then explained that she had been out walking and met a man who was lost. As she asked if she could help, he shared that he had been released from prison that morning and was trying to find his way to the mens' shelter that he had been referred to. My mom looked at the address details of the location he was looking for and quickly confirmed that he was miles away from his intended destination. Rather than send him on his way, she walked him home to our family home and drove him downtown to the facility he was trying to get to. To say I was shocked by her actions would be an understatement, though I knew better than to get upset about her risk-taking. This was who she was, a true community servant.

Initially, I didn't know where to focus my intention to help others and struggled to identify who I could help most with the *Ready to Rise Energy Management System* that I had created. Then I realized that the people who I could help the most were right in front of me—business owners! They were prime candidates because the one thing they sought in pursuing their entrepreneurial dream was freedom. As they poured themselves into building their business, most of them lost control of their life and lost sight of their freedom. With my help and the power of this system, I felt sure that I could help them to turn around their circumstances and realize their freedom.

As an EOS Implementer®, I would regularly work with business owners to help them gain control of their business, increase its value, and get what they wanted from it. As a default, I focused on the business exclusively, and the conversation about what they wanted in life rarely came up. Interestingly, though, when I had the opportunity to ask the question, "What do you really want?" Many business owners didn't know how to answer the question. Some would respond with the desire for "more time" or "more money." But then, when I would persist and dig a little deeper, they all said the same thing—they wanted freedom.

Most of the entrepreneurs I had worked with had become so consumed with running their businesses and keeping up with their family lives that they had long forgotten who they were and what they wanted in life. The elusive concept of freedom, which had led them down the entrepreneurial path in the first place, then became so far out of reach that they preferred not to talk about it. In so many ways, I could relate.

After years of building trust with business owners by helping them take their businesses to the next level, a small number of my clients began expressing their desire to exit their companies. Some wanted to step away from the day-to-day operations and transfer leadership to a successor, while others wanted to sell their business and exit altogether. In each case, they asked me to assist with their transition process. At the time, I had no idea how to help them, but I understood that their personal and financial freedom was at stake, so I committed myself to finding a way to help them prepare for their exit and navigate their transition.

In my research, I discovered a training certification that would teach me the basics of exit planning and equip me to support my clients in the preparation and pursuit of their exit. Within months, I earned the Certified Exit Planning Advisor designation (CEPA), regulated by the Exit Planning Institute, and was ready to step up to the "Owners Box" to guide clients through their exit planning journey. Although there were times that I wondered whether I was good enough to do this work, I would quickly remind myself that for all I lacked in professional experience as a CEPA, I certainly had made up for it with my own personal experience in my "double-exit" from my marriage and business partnership with my ex-husband.

Throughout my own "double exit" journey, I sadly didn't have the right professional representation to protect my interests, I didn't understand the process that I was in, and at no time did the conversation come up about what I wanted. As a result, I experienced catastrophic losses that triggered a deep and dark period in my life. Fuelled by my personal experience and my desire to help set people free, I went to work to build a best-in-class exit planning engagement model that I could use to help business owners unlock their wealth and realize their freedom in business and in life.

When I learned about the unfortunate stories of countless business owners who had lost their wealth, their legacy, and their identity upon exiting their business, I knew it was time to step up and help. The Exit Planning Institute reported that up to 70% of businesses that go to market do not sell, 50% of business exits are involuntary, 75% of business owners regret their decision to exit within 24 months of the sale, and 94% of business owners surveyed did not have a written personal plan for their next chapter. *Shocking*!

I did not want my clients to fall victim to the tragic circumstances of an involuntary exit and risk losing what they valued. It made sense that there could be some benefit in helping them to prepare ahead of time to ensure that they and their business were ready for a future exit and the owner was free to pursue their next chapter of life with confidence. In addition to using the *Value Acceleration Methodology* to address the business and financial aspects of exit planning, I also felt it would be helpful to use the *Ready to Rise Energy Management System* to assist them in preparing themselves for their transition and pursuing their next chapter with confidence.

It was a natural fit because, in the exit planning process, it is important that we factor in the personal, financial, and business goals of the business owner. Only when the business owner understands who they are and what they want in life can we then work with them to align their business with their personal vision and financial goals. When I use this methodology, I can help the owner recognize that they matter most and that the business and future transition needs to align with their goals.

As I started to use the framework with clients, they shared that they loved the simplicity and effectiveness of the system to help them create personal clarity, manage their energy, and systematically take action to move toward their desired life with confidence. Furthermore, they appreciated the fact that the tools were easy to use and maintain throughout their exit planning and transition process. Although I had reservations about sharing my personal journey and system with my clients for fear that they might reject me, the opposite turned out to be true. The more I spoke of my personal struggles and the work I had done to reclaim my identity and rebuild my life, the more they would trust that I could help them navigate their transition journey. I was a living example of the power of this energy management system; it was important that I let them into my life so that they could see what was possible for them.

Whether you are a business owner or any adult navigating a period of personal or professional transition, I applaud you for coming to the table to do the real work—the inner work. As you approach the closing chapters of this book, I also hope you consider opening the companion guide and mini-course included with your purchase to explore the possibilities of what this simple, practical, and sustainable system could unlock for you. You may like to try out a few of the rules and habits, or perhaps a tool or two. My hope is that the *Ready to Rise Energy Management System* will help you to get unstuck and realize your freedom to live your life by your own design.

CHAPTER 14

PULLING IT ALL TOGETHER

To say that personal development and transformation work is difficult and complex would be an understatement. Anyone who has engaged with this level of "inner work" can attest to the fact that it is grueling, confronting, and even terrifying at times. That is not to say that you should not pursue this path forward, but rather, it is a warning that you will need to ensure that you are truly ready to commit to the work because you will be tested and challenged at every stage of the journey. Despite the difficulty of the climb to your personal summit, in every case, the people who dare to rise to the challenge are glad that they did and confirm that life is great at the top.

The reality of the situation is such that we cannot reap the rewards of personal transformation and life re-design without doing the hard work and making the necessary changes to get there. Along the way, it is common to feel frustration and discomfort. These are signs that change is taking place and you are making progress on your journey. Sadly, though, many people misinterpret these symptoms as signs of failure and then use them as an excuse to stop doing the work. If, as you read this, you are experiencing some of these pain points on your own personal development journey, DON'T STOP! These are signs that your efforts are working; you need to keep going!

We are all brought to this work for different reasons, and we are all facing unique circumstances. However, the common theme is that we are facing a fork in the road; we can either embrace change and move toward our freedom, or we can default to our old way of living and keep getting the same frustrating results.

Whether you are in the process of preparing to sell your business, or moving through a major life transition, such as divorce, becoming an empty nester, a career change, or any other life shake-up, this is your time for change. You stand at the foothill of the biggest mountain climb of your life, a climb that will be difficult and challenge you in every way. You may lose friends on the way, and you will be judged for being selfish. But, if you are brave and do the work, the payoff will be high. You will have the opportunity to unlock the real you, create a life that fuels you every day, and embrace the full glory of freedom. Most reasonable adults can appreciate that the changes we want to see in our lives need to start with changes from within us. My own journey has been a good example of that. In fact, I would go so far as to say that my transformation journey only really began after I had owned up to the most difficult truth—I was the problem. Until that time, I had wanted the world to change for me, but in reality, it would not. It was not until I took responsibility for my own happiness and freedom that changes started to take place.

Though I had taken the first step toward change, and I had made a commitment to doing the work necessary to create the life I desired, initially, I struggled to find my path forward until I stumbled across the power of energy management. Learning how to control, manage, and effectively deploy my energy was not easy at first, though with simple disciplines and a whole lot of practice, I started to gain forward momentum.

As you consider your next move on your path to manifest positive changes in your life and pursue your own personal freedom, you will notice that there are no shortages of resources available to you. There are thousands of books and podcasts for you to dive into and endless options of techniques for you to try. Though you will likely find many of them helpful, I anticipate that at some point, you will likely hit a ceiling and feel like nothing is working.

Before giving up, I encourage you to consider trying this simple, practical, and proven *Ready to Rise Energy Management System.*

In bringing this methodology together, I have done my best to make this easy enough to get you started and simple enough to keep you going on your implementation journey. I hope that by now, you will appreciate the value of leveraging the power of systems intelligence to help you simply and effectively upgrade your energy management practice and ultimately upgrade your life. Inside the system, you will find the *5-5-5 Playbook,* containing *5 Rules, 5 Habits,* and 5 Tools, which is then brought together in a 90-day world of planning and execution. As you engage with the materials and the mini-course included with this book, I hope that you will keep it simple, practice often, trust the process, and let the system do the heavy lifting for you.

As you start out on your implementation journey, you may feel tempted to try to go fast. While you can certainly do that, I encourage you to consider taking it slow, as George Morris, a renowned horse trainer and coach, reminds us: *"Slow is smooth. Smooth is fast,"* The data shows that when you slow down and establish a few foundational tools and disciplines, you will likely achieve better and more sustainable results over time.

The fact that you've made it this far through the book tells me that you want more, and perhaps you're considering trying out some of the tools and disciplines we've covered in the preceding pages. Before going any further, I want to make a small disclaimer. Although this system can be powerfully effective, it is important to acknowledge that you've lived with your current approach of thinking, acting, and managing your energy for decades. It will take time to reframe your mind and break many of your old patterns and habits. During the early stages of implementation, there will be times when you feel discomfort and want to give up. Before you do that, I encourage you to take a break and come back to the work when you're ready. It's okay to take a break; just try to avoid stopping altogether. I'm not promising miracles, nor am I guaranteeing results, but if you are truly *Ready to Rise,* I am confident that you will start to see some profound changes within a very short period of time with only a small investment of time and energy.

So what makes the *Ready to Rise Energy Management System* so special and so powerful? Well, I would likely need another chapter or two to fully unpack that. However, I will suffice to say that the secret recipe is made up of three key ingredients. Firstly, the system is simple, which means that it is made up of practical and easy-to-follow tools, rules, and habits so that anyone can use them. Secondly, the system is sustainable, which relates to the fully integrated nature of each of the tools and disciplines within the framework, ensuring that with even the smallest amount of effort, the system can be sustained over time. Lastly, the system is shareable, meaning that you can take what I have provided here within these pages and start using the framework without the help of a paid professional, and even better yet, you can also share it with a friend or spouse and enjoy the journey together.

In the earlier chapters, we learned that freedom can absolutely be a lived experience rather than a destination. We also saw that you can access this lived experience of freedom by simply doing three things well: managing your energy effectively, honoring your true identity, and actively pursuing your desired life. To help amplify this message, I want to share this simple equation to help reinforce the message that freedom is a byproduct of the powerful combination of having both a clear vision and the discipline to execute it. Though vision alone will be helpful, and execution will be beneficial, it is only when these two things are combined and sustained over time that freedom can and will be yours.

Vision + Execution = Freedom

CHAPTER 15

GETTING STARTED

Before we conclude this book, I want to ensure that if you are truly ready for change and willing to take action, you have what you need to get unstuck and take your first step forward toward the freedom you desire. I'll be frank: You have probably tried several different personal development approaches in the past. Likely, some things worked for a short time, but chances are that most of your efforts trailed off. But, just because attempts to change your life have not come together for you in the past, it does not mean you should stop trying. Please know that you don't suck—you are just stuck.

At the very least, I hope this book will elevate your confidence that you can do this. Furthermore, I hope that the way I've explained the *5-5-5 Playbook,* including the *5 Rules, 5 Habits, and 5 Tools*, has given you some level of trust in the power of systems and shown you that you can use a small amount of your energy to affect meaningful and long-lasting changes in your life.

Getting your head and hands around the entirety of this energy management system may feel like a lot to digest all at once, so to help you overcome any lingering barriers to entry, in this chapter, I have proposed an ultra-simple starting place with a sample tool I like to call *The Daily 1-1-1* in the following pages here. The goal here is to give you a taste of what is possible with just five minutes of your time each day.

The Daily 1-1-1

It is quite a simple tool and will only require 3–5 minutes of your morning routine to implement it. I would suggest giving it a try for consecutive days, perhaps seven days to start with. To start with, you will want to situate yourself in a quiet and uninterrupted space before you start your busy day. Then, take a few moments to write down your response to these three prompts:

1. Select one of the *5 Rules* to practice for the day. For your reference, these include: **Be Kind, Be Curious, Be Honest, Be Grateful, Be Humble**. As you choose one of the rules, think about what it means to you and how it will help elevate your mindset and make a positive impact on your day. Write down the mindset rule you will practice throughout the day as a commitment to yourself.
2. Select one of the *5 Habits* to practice for the day. For your reference, these include **Daily Stillness, Solution Focus, Plan Ahead, See Progress, and Playtime**. As you choose one of the habits, consider how it will help you increase your productivity and satisfaction by the end of the day. Write down the habit you will practice throughout the day as a commitment to yourself.
3. Think about all the things you could do in the day, or perhaps the things you feel you should do in the day. Select one thing you want to prioritize taking action on for no one else's benefit but your own. Give yourself permission to be selfish and put your item at the top of the list for the day so that by nightfall, you will have the satisfaction of knowing that you mattered today. Write down your commitment to doing that one thing.
4. Lastly, at the end of the day, when all of your work is done and you prepare yourself for bed, pull out *The Daily 1-1-1* and reflect upon your progress made that day.

5. Repeat the next day and the next for 7 days. Notice the impact this has on your day-to-day life.

As I shared earlier, making changes to our behavior and working on our system for living can seem simple in theory, but it is not easy in practice. You may even find this little exercise difficult to maintain for seven days. As you work with it, I encourage you to practice kindness and stay open to this humbling journey. If personal transformation and life redesign were easy, everyone would already be well on their way. Start small, keep it simple, and keep going.

Take this opportunity to get started with the ***My Life Assessment and The Daily 1-1-1 tool today by scanning the QR code featured at the back of this book.*** This link will also unlock your full companion guide and digital mini-course to ensure that you have everything you need to rise to your own summit.

DAILY 1-1-1 🎁

ONE MINDSET RULE TO REINFORCE TODAY

ONE PRACTICAL HABIT TO PRACTICE TODAY

ONE HIGH PRIORITY ACTION TO TAKE TODAY

BRIEF EVENING REFLECTION FROM THE DAY

CHAPTER 16

SELF ASSESSMENT

Before taking this any further, I believe it's important for you to take a moment to ask yourself why you might want to pursue this inward path and to identify the ways in which your life could improve through doing this inner work. Understanding why this is important to you will help you establish buy-in to the process of working on yourself and your life.

My goal is to help you build a strong enough case for you to give it a try because once you start working on yourself and your life in a meaningful way. Whether you decide to go all in on this journey or would rather start with a trial run, it's important to acknowledge that the climb to reach your personal summit will be difficult and uncomfortable at times, but the payoff will be high. Initially, this work will feel like a big investment of time and energy. There will be times that you will question your judgment, experience frustration, and want to pack it in. That's why it's crucial to have a strong reason why you might want to start this work before you get going.

My hope is that you will identify that there is a space between where you are now and where you want to get to in your life. I hope by now you will understand that doing the same thing over and expecting a different result is not only frustrating but also insane. In order to get out of your slump and move forward toward that life you desire, change will have to start with you.

The challenge is that when we are in our circumstances, we can often lose clarity and objectivity. Some days we think we are doing well, then other days we think we suck. It can be helpful to step outside of our system to assess how we are doing and then use that outside perspective to identify opportunities for change. Although energy itself can be difficult to measure because it is intangible, it is possible to assess how well we are managing our energy by assessing some key areas of our life that will show us how we are doing and clearly show us areas for improvement.

With this in mind, I thought it might be helpful to share with you a bonus tool to help you assess the strength of your current energy management system. The *My Life Assessment* is a simple 20-question tool that is designed to get you asking yourself some foundational questions related to your current energy management practices and identify the areas that you could start to make some small but important changes to your daily practices in an effort to help you get more of what you want out of your present and future life.

Each of the 20 questions can be answered on a scale of 1-5, with 5 being great, and your total score out of 100 will then give you a sense of how well you are managing your energy. I have also shared some thoughts about how to interpret your score with the "Understanding Your Score" notes section in the pages that follow. For each of the three ranges of results, I have shared some guidance on what you might like to start your work on to upgrade your system.

My goal in sharing this bonus assessment tool is to help you understand what 100% strong looks like and incentivize you to start your implementation journey so that you can upgrade the strength of your system on a journey toward 100% strength and get more of what you want out of your life—freedom!

"Upgrade your system, upgrade your life."
– Renee Russo

Take this opportunity to get started with the My Life Assessment today by scanning the QR code featured at the back of this book. This link will also unlock your full companion guide and digital mini-course to ensure that you have everything you need to rise to your own summit.

My Life Assessment

The *My Life Assessment* is designed to enable you to step out of your current reality so that you can objectively evaluate how well you are currently managing your energy, assess how aligned your actions are with your desires for your life, identify the level of clarity about your personal vision, and then rate the level of freedom you are experiencing across the five pillars of freedom. After completing the assessment, you will have a clear understanding of the overall strength of your energy management system and better understand how you can use the *Ready to Rise Energy Management System* to upgrade your system and upgrade your life.

For each statement on the assessment, rate yourself and your way of living in the context of the question on a scale of 1 to 5, with 1 being the lowest and 5 being the highest. In this case, a 1 would indicate an "absolute no," a 5 would indicate an "absolute yes," and a 3 would indicate "somewhat." Then, tally up your total responses and use the interpretation scale after the assessment to help you understand what it means.

By reflecting on these key areas, you will gain a much clearer understanding of how this simple, practical, and proven energy management system will help you more effectively manage your energy, unlock your true identity, and realize your freedom to live life by your own design. You may also be able to more confidently determine if you are ready to take action and meaningfully work on yourself and your life with the *Ready to Rise Energy Management System.*

MY LIFE ASSESSMENT

NAME: _____   DATE: _____

INSTRUCTIONS:

For each statement, rate yourself and your current personal practice on a scale of 1 to 5, with 1 being the lowest and 5 being the highest. In this case, a 1 would indicate an "absolute no," a 5 would indicate an "absolute yes," and a 3 would indicate "somewhat." Then, tally up your total responses and use the interpretation scale below to help you understand what they mean and identify opportunities to upgrade your energy management system.

QUESTIONS:	1	2	3	4	5
I am clear on my reason for being in this life and align my personal and professional life with this inner purpose.	○	○	○	○	○
I am clear on my personal values and filter my personal and professional relationships based on them.	○	○	○	○	○
I manage my financial resources so that I can invest time and money into the activities that elevate my quality of life.	○	○	○	○	○
I maintain regular health practices that elevate my physical health.	○	○	○	○	○
I maintain a student mindset and engage with enriching sources of learning on a regular basis.	○	○	○	○	○
I consistently make time for daily introspection to align with myself and focus on what matters most to me.	○	○	○	○	○
I consistently spend time looking ahead to prioritize what is most important to me, and I begin with the end in mind.	○	○	○	○	○
I create space in my life for play to enjoy exploration and adventure to help me connect with my inner child.	○	○	○	○	○
I embrace the challenges in my life with a solution-based mentality. I focus on what I control and take action.	○	○	○	○	○
I appreciate and recognize the good in my life and allow myself to receive joy because I am worthy.	○	○	○	○	○

MY LIFE ASSESSMENT

QUESTIONS:

RATING SCALE: 1 2 3 4 5

- I recognize efforts and reflect on the progress made towards my goals and objectives on a consistent basis.
- I avoid making assumptions and judgments about myself and others, and instead, I practice a curious mindset.
- I practice giving honest feedback to myself and others without hesitation because it is the right thing to do.
- I embrace the beautiful imperfections of all humans and meet people where they are with compassion.
- I fight like I am right, listen like I am wrong, and understand that failure is a critical part of learning.
- I have a clear picture of what my desired life looks like ten years from now, and I focus my energy towards it.
- I resist the need to be all things and focus on making an impact by doing what I am truly best at.
- I practice a rhythm of personal goal-setting and prioritize my action plans to help me execute my goals.
- I leverage restorative health practices that increase my, physical, emotional and spiritual well-being.
- I trust that in order make the impact I seek to have in the world, I must first take care of myself first.

COUNT

SUM

TOTAL

Understanding Your Score:

1-40: Indicates significant opportunities for personal growth and development. It's an ideal time to engage deeply with the *Ready to Rise Energy Management System*. Definitely consider downloading the free companion guide and enrolling in our mini-course. You have nothing to lose and everything to gain.

41-70: Shows good foundational practices with room for targeted improvement. You will improve your ability to focus and manage energy by deepening your mindset and habit practices. Also, the *5 Tools* will help you focus your current planning and execution practices in a more targeted and integrated way. Consider downloading the free companion guide and enrolling in our mini-course. With a bit more refinement, you will notice big improvements.

71-100: You already have a strong energy management foundation and a solid practice of setting and pursuing your goals. With a more integrated and holistic approach, you will surely access higher levels of performance and increase your capacity to truly live life by your own design. You are doing great work already. With the companion guide, online mini-course, and a conversation with one of our coaches, you will have the opportunity to get everything you want in both business and in life.

Note: I recommend taking this assessment every 90 days to allow yourself to see your progress on your self-discovery journey. This exercise is not intended to trigger self-judgment or self-loathing. It is simply a tool to help you initiate an inner dialogue about what is working and not working in your life. Then, identify ways in which some of the practices you read about in this book could help you elevate your energy and your life.

CONCLUSION

They say that the definition of insanity is doing the same thing over and over again and expecting a different result. Sadly, throughout my life, I found myself repeating unhealthy patterns of people-pleasing and self-sacrificing behavior that I hoped would one day bring me joy and fulfillment in my life. Instead, these behaviors caused me to sink deeper into isolation and depression. Somehow, I thought that if I tried harder and found new ways to make others happy, I would one day feel some of that happiness for myself. Though, no matter how hard I tried, I kept coming up short. By all accounts, I was most certainly insane.

After many years of running from myself into the needs of others, I had become so accustomed to living for the sake and benefit of others that I started to lose sight of my own identity and dreams for my future. While on the surface, I behaved as though I was happy, the truth was that on the inside, I felt imprisoned, frustrated, and desperate to break free. As I approached my 40th birthday, I found that I could no longer hold up the false front that everything was fine, and I finally, at last, owned up to my truth—I was not happy. I wanted to break free from my unhealthy marriage, and I wanted to break out of the inner prison that I had been locked up in for so long.

The path to pursue my double exit—from our marriage and our business—quickly became hostile, and after a long and futile battle, I gave in. I left my wealth on the table and took the one thing I wanted all along—my freedom. Sadly, along the way, I also lost my children, my home, my community, and my identity, which sent me into a sharp downward spiral.

In the depths of my despair, I received a much-needed wake-up call while saving the life of another human being. This experience helped me realize that I was ready to get back up from my fall and do the hard work to rebuild my life. Though the climb up the mountain ahead of me to reclaim my identity and redesign my life would be steep and treacherous, I was committed to the journey and started the hard work to climb to my summit.

With a fire lit inside me and a renewed sense of urgency to get my life back on track, I understood that I would need tools and resources to help me navigate my climb, and so began my discovery journey into the world of energy management. Before long, I had curated a small number of tools and disciplines that I put into practice to help me learn how to focus my mind, manage my energy, and prioritize the things that mattered to me.

In the process of learning how to manage my energy and build healthier lifestyle habits, I developed my own version of an energy management system, comprising the *5-5-5 Playbook*, which included *5 Tools, 5 Rules,* and *5 Habits.* With practice and consistency, over time, I found that I was able to break my past toxic patterns, elevate my energy levels, and eventually pursue the tough climb ahead to rebuild my life.

In the process of working with my energy, I developed strong foundations of self-discipline, which then revealed itself to be the greatest form of self-love. For the first time in my life, I not only mattered, but I mattered most. With this renewed sense of love and care for myself, I then bravely started the work to re-discover my true identity that I had held captive for so long. Then, over time, as I learned how to be myself again, I found that my passion for life increased, and the dreams for a big, beautiful life that I had stowed away as a young girl returned.

Though overwhelming to think about at first, with the help of simple personal visioning tools that I adapted from my business strategy resources, I was soon able to clearly define my core identity, my *10-Year Vision* for my life, my 3-Year *Painted Picture*, and the Big Goals that would move me forward toward the life I desired. It felt great.

Although there were times that I struggled with feelings of guilt and shame for being so selfish, I would quickly remind myself of all of the reasons why my exit was the right thing to do. One of the driving forces for me became the desire to become the example of an empowered, elevated, and independent adult that I wanted for them. It seemed that if I wanted a beautiful life of freedom and fulfillment for my children, I would need to first model that for myself.

Along my climb toward my personal summit in search of my freedom, I experienced an amazing realization that the freedom that I had been seeking all along had been hiding in plain sight. I realized that the freedom I sought was not a destination but a living experience, and the only thing standing between me and my freedom was myself. For decades, I had been working against myself, denying my own needs while hiding in the expectations of others and enslaving myself to our business. Looking back on my journey, I could see that I had denied myself the freedom that I once desired because I did not feel worthy of it, and I feared that I might seem selfish. Then, as I broke free of the shackles I had put myself in, I experienced the freedom to be myself and walk my own path each day. I discovered that freedom was simply the byproduct of choosing me.

Whether you are a leader moving through a career transition, a spouse moving through divorce, or a business owner moving through the process of selling your business, it is reasonable to expect that you may be feeling disorientated, disconnected, and somewhat immobilized in the difficulty of your transition. Moving through significant personal and professional change can be particularly hard when you are struggling to manage your energy, having a hard time remembering who you really are, and feeling unsure about what you really want.

It is likely that you have tried a number of different therapies, techniques, workshops, and approaches to help you navigate through this difficult phase.

Though you are doing your best and trying hard to make changes, you probably feel like it is not working, or at least it is a lot harder than it needs to be. Please listen closely to this statement: you don't suck, you are just stuck. The truth is that your system for managing your energy and living your life is designed to get the results it gets. Therefore, if you truly want to upgrade your life, you need to start first by upgrading your system for managing your energy.

It is my hope that in witnessing my journey, you will feel reassured that you are not alone in your current challenges and frustration with yourself and your life. Furthermore, I hope that you will feel encouraged that you, too, can transform your life and pursue your *Significant Life* of freedom. I can attest that it won't be easy, but I can assure you it will be worth it. With every painful step forward on your climb toward your own mountain summit, you will get closer to discovering who you really are and what you desire in this life. As you approach your summit, you will realize your freedom to live your own version of your *Significant Life*.

Within these pages, I have shared all the tools, disciplines, and insights I gathered on my mission to crack the code of energy management and help set people like you free. As you explore the free gifts that come with your purchase, including the companion guide, mini-course, and *My Life Assessment* bonus tool, please know that I have done my very best to try to make the system easy enough for you to get started and simple enough for you to maintain over time. You may want to dive into the work quickly, but I encourage you to take it slow and gradually embrace everything the *Ready to Rise Energy Management System* has to offer over time.

As we bring this time together to a close, I hope that in making your way through this book, you will have gained some meaningful insights that will help you take positive steps forward to pursue your freedom to be yourself and live your life by your own design. You are so worthy of all that you desire—truly, you are. With this entire framework now in your hands, I'll draw upon the wisdom of my yoga guru, Shakti Mhi, and say to you, "I am not your guru. The guru is within you." The simple truth is that the change you want to see in your life will come from changes you make within yourself. The only person who can truly elevate you out of your circumstances and help you realize the freedom you crave is you. Although the path ahead may feel daunting right now, the only question you need to ask yourself is: *Am I Ready to Rise?*

There's a mountain climb ahead of you and a summit with your name on it. It won't be an easy journey, but it will be worth it. Your path to realizing your freedom awaits. When you are ready to rise, I'll meet you at the top. See you soon!!

APPENDIX

This appendix serves as a practical resource to complement the strategies discussed in the book. You are encouraged to adapt these tools to fit your personal needs and revisit them regularly to stay on track with your goals. *All of these tools are available in more depth by scanning the QR code at the beginning and end of this book.*

1. Daily Focuser (Page 64)

The *Daily Focuser* helps you connect with your inner self at the beginning of each day. It provides you with the opportunity to clarify your top priorities for the day and ensure that you start the day in control of both your mind and behavior. At the end of the day, the tool also provides space to reflect on and recognize your progress.

- **How to use the tool:** Make a positive self-affirming statement about yourself to get yourself in a positive headspace. Then, choose one of the *5 Rules* to establish a positive mindset for the day. Next, select one of the *5 Habits* to work on for the day, remembering that habits build capacity. Once you have your commitments set, then take the time to prioritize the top 3 most important tasks that you want to complete for yourself that day. In the evening, take the time to reflect on your accomplishments and jot down your progress. Any incomplete items may be re-prioritized the following day or later in the week.

2. 90-Day Driver (Page 76)

This *90-Day Driver* tool facilitates personal quarterly planning and goal setting every 90-day period. Through the process of setting targets, Rocks, and focused objectives for the quarter, you will have the opportunity to gain traction toward your annual *Big Goals* and personal freedoms of growth, health, and people relationships.

- **How to use the tool:** Begin by setting a "connect to the core" statement to reaffirm your core values, core purpose, and core talents, as referenced in your *My Life Design*. Then, set up to three targets that relate to your annual measurable targets. Proceed to set up to three Rocks that will help you gain traction toward your *Big Goals* identified for the year. Then finally, personal priorities around the freedom of growth, health, and people relationships.

3. Weekly Planner (Page 84)

The Weekly Planner offers the opportunity to practice the habit of planning ahead, which can help you start the week out on the front foot. The tools also provide the opportunity to stay on track toward your 90-day plan with weekly prioritized action planning. The tool can also help you to stay in a mind space of gratitude and self-appreciation while also helping to ensure that your personal growth, health, and relationship objectives are prioritized each week.

- **How to use the tool::** Start out by forming a gratitude and self-appreciation statement to get you in a positive mind space. Then, identify milestone efforts that will help you to move toward your 3 Rocks outlined on your *90-Day Driver*. Finally, identify a small number of objectives for personal growth, health, and relationships to be actioned throughout the week ahead. At the end of the week, review your accomplishments and note down your progress.

4. My Life Design (Page 106-107)

The *My Life Design* tool helps you to identify who you are, why you are here, where you want to go, and how you plan to get there. This tool is designed to put you in control of your life and help you to ensure that everything you do is in alignment with who you are and where you are going, recognizing that you matter most.

- **How to use the tool:** Take your time to go on a self-discovery journey to understand your core identity, capture the essence of who you are, why you are here, and what you are naturally good at with a statement for each of your core values, your core purpose, and your core talents. Create and envision a future for yourself with your *10-Year Vision* and your 3-Year *Painted Picture*. Then, identify your execution plan with your annual targets and *Big Goals* for the year. As issues of future ideas come up, capture them in the *Think Tank* for future consideration; this will help to avoid having them show up in your 2 a.m. thoughts!

5. Freedom Check-Up (Page 130-131)

The *Freedom Check-Up* is designed to get you thinking about what each of the five pillars of personal freedom could mean to you in your life. This is not intended to be aspirational. Each of the definitions of freedoms should be related to how you would like to be living your day-to-day life if you were free to be yourself and live your life as you pleased.

- **How to use the tool:** Take the time to consider each of the freedoms one at a time. Start by asking yourself what living with the *Freedom of People* could look like for you if you were free to choose to surround yourself with people who aligned with your core values and how that would impact the quality of your life. Move to the next *Freedom of Purpose* and describe what living and working in alignment with your core purpose would look like and how that would impact your life.

Move to the *Freedom of Growth* and describe what honoring this desire for personal development would look like for you and how that would impact your life. Take time to think about what the *Freedom of Wealth* could look like for you if you were able to exceed your basic needs for living and use your resources for a positive impact. Lastly, take time to define what the *Freedom of Health* could look like for you if you were able to prioritize your holistic well-being and take care of your health on a regular basis. Once defined, assess yourself on a scale of 1-10, with 10 being highest, and identify opportunities to elevate your lived experience of freedom.

6. The Daily 1-1-1 (Page 152)

The Daily 1-1-1 tool is a bonus tool designed to give you a small taste test of the power of daily energy management. In just three minutes a day, the tool can help you increase your focus and improve your ability to prioritize your needs every day.

- **How to use the tool:** Draw *5 Rules* to form a positive mindset rule to practice throughout the day. Next, choose from the *5 Habits* a positive behavior to practice throughout the day. Then, identify one high-priority personal task to accomplish by the end of the day. Lastly, at the end of the day, take one minute to note down your progress and any impact on your energy and confidence levels.

7. My Life Assessment (Page 156-157)

The *My Life Assessment* bonus tool is designed to give you the ability to step outside your current system and assess how well you are managing energy and realizing your freedom. This qualitative and quantifiable assessment of your system for living can help you identify areas for improvement and also recognize your improvements over time as you integrate the *Ready to Rise Energy Management System* into your day-to-day life.

- **How to use the tool:** Review each of the 20 questions and evaluate your current state on a scale of 1-5. Add up your total score and review the "Understanding Your Score" guidance for suggestions on how to increase your results in the next 90-day period. You may also like to go back through your responses and prioritize some of your actions around the questions that scored in the range of 1-3. Consider taking the assessment every 90-day period so that you can observe your progress.

ABOUT THE AUTHOR

Renee Russo is a high-energy change-maker obsessed with setting business owners free. As an Expert EOS Implementer®, Certified Exit Planning Advisor (CEPA), Speaker, Author, and Facilitator, Renee and her team help business owners gain control of their companies, unlock their wealth, and realize their freedom to live life by design.

After a series of catastrophic life events triggered by the "double exit" from her marriage and business, Renee fell hard. At her breaking point, she faced a difficult decision: Was she going to get back up or fall to her demise?

Deciding to rise from this final fall, Renee bravely began the steep climb up the mountain to reclaim herself and rebuild her life. She quickly understood that this was not going to be an easy climb, but with nothing to lose, she courageously took up the challenge because, for the first time in her life, she felt she was worth it.

In the early stages of her inward personal development journey, Renee realized that many of the techniques and approaches she had tried in the past hadn't worked because she was not ready to take it seriously, and also, her approach was designed to fail. One of the flaws in her approach was that her mindset, her behaviors, and her goals were not in alignment. Secondly, she was trying to do too many things at once and had overwhelmed herself. Then, when she unlocked the power of systems intelligence and the need to keep it all simple, she finally started to gain some forward momentum on her path to rebuilding her life.

Drawing from her business coaching toolkit and her self-help book library, Renee set about testing and curating a small set of simple and practical tools and disciplines that she could use to coach herself through her transformational journey. She applied design thinking concepts, tried many things, failed many times, and eventually distilled a simple, practical, and systemized personal energy management system that gave her the capacity to reclaim her identity, rebuild her life, and realize her freedom.

Readers of Renee's book *Ready to Rise* can now affordably access the entire *Ready to Rise Energy Management System* that she used to turn her tragic circumstances around for the better. Within the pages of the book, she openly shares with readers the full *5-5-5 Playbook,* containing *the 5 Rules, 5 Habits,* and *5 Tools* so that they can self-implement the system and build their own 90-day world of personal planning and pursue their own transformation journey with confidence.

Renee holds nothing back from her audience. She is a true go-giver who generously shares all that she has learned with those who are *Ready to Rise* up and realize their freedom to live their life by their own design.

ACKNOWLEDGMENTS

Everything that I have ever read, studied, or listened to throughout my life has built the inventory of information, insights, and intellect that I have gathered to date. With that in mind, I acknowledge that many of the concepts and ideas shared throughout these pages will likely seem familiar, especially if you and I enjoy many of the same authors and thought leaders. Frankly, there are so many people that I would like to mention. However, that might require another 100 pages, so instead, I will do my best to focus on the key sources of inspiration that helped me put together these words and the *Ready To Rise Energy Management System.*

May I start out by saying that I am profoundly thankful for the authors and thought leaders whose work has shaped me as a human being and also as a professional speaker and facilitator. Many of you taught me new things, and others helped me put words to the thoughts swimming around inside my head. The most wonderful thing that each of you incredible beings gave me was company and connection, which was particularly important to me in my darkest hours.

It gives me great pleasure to share some special acknowledgments to the creators who have inspired and impacted me most in writing this book.

- Gino Wickman: Your example and your book *Traction* have profoundly impacted my understanding of the power of systems thinking and given me the tools to change my life for the better.

- Dan Sullivan: Your *Strategic Coach* program and many thinking tools have helped me recognize my progress and embrace the potential for freedom in my life.
- Simon Sinek: Your book *Find Your Why* and online videos have helped me to discover my purpose and share that same gift of discovery with many people.
- Stephen Covey: Your book *The 7 Habits of Highly Effective People* was one of the first personal development books I read at 21, and it continues to reinforce the power of personal habits as a source for positive change.
- Miguel Ruiz: Your book *The Four Agreements* has helped me to understand and share with others the power of the mind and the link between these principles and wholesome living.
- Shakti Mhi: Your training and your book *The Enigma of Self-Realization* has shown me the power of the inner work.

Thank you all for being part of my journey. Your influence and inspiration have helped shape the person I am today, and for that, I am eternally grateful.

DOWNLOAD YOUR FREE GIFTS

When you scan this QR code, you will have instant access to the free companion guide and mini-course to help you get started right away. Also, the *My Life Assessment* will give you a pulse on the strength of your current energy management system and give you a clear sense of the opportunity at hand for you to upgrade your system and upgrade your life.

Scan the QR code:

I appreciate your interest in my book and value your feedback as it helps me improve future versions. I would appreciate it if you could leave your invaluable review on Amazon.com with your feedback. Thank you!

Manufactured by Amazon.ca
Bolton, ON